MW00943211

Life With Extra Cheese

Being the ham in the sandwich generation

Heather Davis,

Bestselling, award-winning author of
Oversharing My Life

Also by Heather Davis

Oversharing My Life

Getting Lucky

Crazy On Board

Girlfriend Rules

We're Not The Cleavers

LIFE WITH EXTRA CHEESE. Copyright © 2015 by Heather Davis.
All Rights Reserved. Printed in the United States of America. For information, contact Road Trip Media, LLC (RoadTripMediaLLC@gmail.com).

Davis, Heather.
    Life With Extra Cheese / Heather Davis.—1st Road Trip Media, LLC
        ISBN: 978-1512377729

    1.   American wit and humor
    2.   Sandwich generation

Cover design by Brandy Walker of Sister Sparrow Graphic Design.

No part of this book may be used or reproduced in any manner whosoever without written permission of the copyright owner except in the case of brief quotations embodied in articles or reviews of this specific work.

To my own momma—
thank you for your support always;
glad I can return the favor

If evolution really works,
how come mothers
only have two hands?
-*Milton Berle*

Let's Start At The Very Beginning

I glanced at my phone as we were heading out the door to church. It was my sister. A small voice inside my head whispered that I shouldn't answer it. My sister is a little bit of a panicker. Once my niece had a mole appear behind her ear, and Rachel, my sister, called me convinced that her precious little three-year-old had developed a rare skin condition, probably contagious. The mole "disappeared" during the evening bath, so all was well once again, but there for a while it was very touch and go. I believe she may have filled out the Make-A-Wish papers before that fateful bath.

I ignored the voice, though. I would sanctimoniously announce that her child was perfect and that the inch-and-a-half of ice that was on the ground would eventually melt (it was raining ice pellets), and I would tell her that I had to go help with Sunday school, so her early morning call had better be important.

"Yes, I know the weather's bad," I answered.

"Mom's had a stroke."

"What?" I gasped. "How do you know?"

"She called 9-1-1, and we heard it on the scanner." (If you've read my other books, you'll already know this; if you haven't then you'll soon find out that our family has an affinity for emergency services scanners. Also? You should read my books. Look me up on Amazon or shoot me an email. I can hook ya up with a real good price!)

"Maybe it's not a stroke," I offered.

"They're taking her to the hospital."

"Can y'all get in?" I asked her. She lived about twenty-minutes south of town. We lived five minutes from the hospital.

"I think so."

"I'll meet you there."

I hung up the phone, but the panic in my sister's voice was still ringing in my ears. And, this time, it was justified.

But wait; that's not the *very* beginning ...

Let's Start At The Very, Very Beginning

On Thursdays, I meet with my writer friends. Two of us have moms who seemed to make it a habit to always call us on Thursdays, forgetting that we have this very important ~~gossip~~ critique meeting. My mom is one of those moms.

Almost every single Thursday, she'd call me during the meeting. Usually she called just to chat. So the last Thursday in February when the four of us sat around Marilyn's dining room table and talked about ~~the social injustices in our community~~ our writing, my phone rang. I saw that it was my mom and sent it to voice mail. I'd call her when I left Marilyn's.

A little bit later, she called again. I legitimately didn't hear the call. (Yes, the phone was on silent ... what's your point?)

I left Marilyn's a little bit before ten. I listened to my voice mail first:

Hi Heather. I just wanted to call you and tell you not to worry. Your sister is all worried about me, but it's not a big deal. I just, ya know, had a bad headache today. That's all.

It was totally weird that my sister hadn't called me as well, since she's a panicker. (It's a word.) So, I called her.

"Well," Rachel took a deep breath and began tattle-telling, "today, she met us at McGaggles and ate a cheeseburger, then she had a headache, and I gave her two Tylenols, and then she went home and slept for a really long time." She took a breath again.

"She's seventy-five. You just described a very full day for a seventy-five year old." I tried to calm my panicky sister.

"Yeah, but she slept for like five hours and then she woke up and her blood sugar was almost 200 and her blood pressure was really low."

"Okay," I sighed. "I'll call her."

I tapped my favorite contacts then tapped my mom's face. It rang and rang and rang and rang. I hung up without leaving a message.

I tapped my mom's other face—her landline. (She's seventy-five-years-old. Old habits die hard.) No answer. I did leave a message.

Heading home, I called Brian and explained that my sister was panicking because she may have poisoned mom with acetaminophen and now my mom was not answering her phone.

"I probably need to go check on her," I finished my explanation with a sigh, then turned on the main thoroughfare in our town and drove to my mom's house.

She returned my call at the exact moment I turned into her driveway.

After she explained the same basic events of the day that my sister had, I encouraged her to go to her doctor on Friday.

"And say what?" she questioned me, as she always does when I offer her any suggestions.

"That you had low blood pressure, high blood sugar and you slept for five hours in the middle of the day. Just to get it on record that you had a wonky day." I'm sure that wonky is a medical term.

She didn't go see the doctor.

Saturday, she wasn't feeling bad, but she wasn't feeling great.

Sunday morning, she called 9-1-1 for herself. She recognized that she was having a stroke.

Oh Be Careful, Little Mouth, What You Say

Instead of going to church that fateful Sunday, my husband carefully drove me over the piling ice to the hospital. We beat the ambulance—they had farther to come. I gingerly walked across the frozen parking lot when the ambulance arrived. My sister, who had the farthest of all of us to come, wouldn't arrive for another half hour.

I called Aunt Kay, my mom's sister, and told her that my mom might have had a stroke and that I was at the hospital waiting to see her. She called their brothers. I posted on Facebook, asking for prayers. By the end of the day, I had over two hundred responses.

(I have over one thousand friends—I'm still peeved about the other eight hundred of you.)

(Not Really.)

Prior to my sister arriving, I quizzed my mom.
What were you doing when you called 9-1-1?
Do you know where you are, Mom?
What's the year?
Who's the president?
Do you know who I am?

She was surprisingly coherent. She had all the right answers. This was more than I could say for her prior to that Sunday morning. Prior to that day, if you asked her what kind of car she drove, her answer would have been a light-colored one. She drives a silver Honda Odyssey.

(Drives? *Drives*? Drove. Past tense. Let me just cut to the chase: She no longer drives.)

The ER staff shuttled her in and out of that curtained cubby no less than a dozen times doing one test or another on her. My uncle John, also known as my wise ol' uncle from the south, called to check in. He was in St. Louis with my aunt Liz, who was having a kidney transplant that week. My aunt Carolyn called to check in. My aunt Kay called to check in. Sweet friends from my mom's church stopped by despite the fact that the ice continued to fall from the grey sky to the frozen ground.

My phone continued to ding with texts from friends and family. It buzzed with updates from Facebook with concern for my momma. It rang when Brian phoned just to check on me.

"What are you doing?" My mom said, my thumbs furiously typing updates to those who requested them.

"I just took a picture of you in your hospital gown, and I'm posting it to Instagram."

"Well," she said, her voice weak and her face tired, "As long as you don't post it on Facebook."

She was, and still is, a very active share-er on Facebook. She had a reputation to uphold.

My mother had the wherewithal to have the paramedics grab her purse before they left the house, so while my mom was off getting some sort of test, my sister and I sifted through it and pulled her insurance cards out and registered her with the hospital. We were just finishing up when the nurses brought my mom back to the room.

The E.R. doctor, whose name was something akin to Bubba, came in and announced that the hospital didn't have an MRI technician on call, so they couldn't do an MRI until Monday. "So," he concluded, "we can't seem to find anything wrong with her."

She couldn't move her right hand or arm. She couldn't move her right leg or foot. She had lost complete control over her bowels and her bladder. Her face was visibly drawn and her voice was weak.

My mouth dropped open when the doctor continued, "If we can't find anything wrong with her, we can't really keep her, I guess."

I felt my sister's face turn toward mine.

"What will we do?" she whispered, her most prominent emotion—her fear—evident in her voice.

My most prominent emotion at that exact moment was pissed-off'ed-ness. Was he really saying there was nothing wrong with the woman who was now uncontrollably crying on the hospital gurney, insisting she had no idea why she was crying? Was he really saying that the woman whose right arm continued to fall off the bed because she had no control over it was okay? Was he really saying that he wouldn't, at the very least, admit her for observation?

I let my emotion lead my words and melt into the room. "We'll just take her to my house." And that, my friends, is all that my mom remembers most about the day she had a stroke. (Not really, but close enough.)

Not In My Plans

I like to imagine that the ER nurse pulled Dr. Jim Bob to the side and said, "Dude!" as she slapped him upside the head, knocking some sense into him. The next time he came into the room, he said they were planning on admitting her, and she could see the neurologist on Monday. She'd been in the hospital for over six hours at this point.

I was almost forty-four. My sister was almost forty. But, when I looked at her sitting beside me in that curtain-walled room, I saw a much younger version of my sister.

ееееееее

She was three years old when our dad had his first heart attack. I was seven. Two years later, he had another heart attack and then faced open-heart surgery. I remember sitting at the dinner table one night before we went to Tulsa for the big surgery, and my daddy telling us that he never wanted to be kept alive by machines.

In my little kid mind, I imagined that some robot, looking much like R2D2 from Star Wars, continuing to perform CPR on my dad so he wouldn't die.

When my dad had his first stroke almost ten years after his first heart attack, he said the same thing, "I don't want any damn machines keeping me alive."

He also told us that he didn't want us to have a funeral for him because they were too expensive. He wanted to be cremated and then tossed to the side.

At the age of sixteen, I knew my dad's exact plans for his end-of-life. And with each health event that we paced through with my dad, my sister looked exactly the same. She looked like the three year old, tow-headed scared little girl. Regardless of how old she really was.

At the age of sixty-nine, my dad had his final heart attack and final stroke. Having no brain activity at all, we removed him from the life support machines—which looked nothing like R2D2—and three days later, he died. My sister was almost twenty-eight at the time. She looked like she was three.

My mom's plans were very different, though.

They were very different because we never talked about them. I had some ideas, though. I wanted my mom to die when she was ninety-nine years old, peacefully in her sleep in her own home having gone to bed the night before with a sound mind. I wanted her to have her hands crossed on her chest and fresh daisies beside her bed. I wanted the neighborhood birds to be perched above her bedroom window whistling "It Is Well With My Soul."

I wanted my mom to die in a Disney movie, apparently. My way still beats being trampled by wildebeests for sure.

llllllll

As I sat in the emergency room wondering why they didn't just catheterize my mom's bladder already, I realized that all of my plans were changing.

My younger daughter, who had just turned ten, had just joined a competitive softball team. Her schedule was slam-packed with practices, travel and tournaments. My older daughter, who was twelve, was on the middle school golf team and played cello in the orchestra. Not that there's any good time for a stroke to happen, but now was really *not* a good time as far as I was concerned. I didn't ask my mom, but I'm sure she would have agreed.

We didn't have to take my mom to our house that day. She was admitted. I didn't have to go all Macgyver and catheterize her myself with a drinking straw, brightly-patterned duct tape and a Ziploc baggie. I didn't go home that night. I didn't sleep that night.

I did eat a McGaggle's cheeseburger at about nine o'clock that night. My mom looked over at me from her hospital bed and said, "You know that's how this all started."

My Mom and Amy Winehouse

Within the next few days, my mom received an MRI, had an EKG, performed very well on her EEG as well as all the other letters of the alphabet. She met with a neurologist, got a catheter, drank a liquid diet, and had her vitals checked every three minutes or so. Maybe a little bit longer.

The good news: The neurologist was beyond excited to see her awake, aware and speaking. Her stroke had occurred in such a place that rendered her without the use of her right side. It also typically rendered its victim speechless and with limited memory, which my mom didn't seem to be afflicted with. Often times, he said, they slept and had a difficult time staying awake. My mom was doing well—except for the physical inflictions.

We moved her to rehab. She did not say no, no, no. Her first rehab placement was in the hospital on the rehab floor. This really disturbed my younger daughter, Briley. She didn't even know that her Nana had a drug problem. I explained to her that people receive rehab for all sorts of reasons.

Aunt Kay came up and stayed around until we got mom settled in rehab. She was good to have around—she thought the doctor was a patient and tried to kick him out of the rehab room. I had to explain rehab to her as well.

The rules on rehab are much more strict than the rules on a regular ol' floor. Basically, we couldn't see my mom until the afternoon when the therapies were completed. She received intensive occupational therapy and physical therapy that kept her tied up for a big part of the day.

This was a blessing in disguise for me. My daughter, Briley, was balling. We were already juggling the girls' activities. I had a frozen shoulder and was going to physical therapy twice a week, and Brian had just started a new teaching position and was learning a new curriculum. Oh! And I was finishing book four of a four-book publishing contract. (Have you read them? Go get them now— TMI Mom.) I found myself saying, on more than one occasion, that this was really a bad time for my mom to have a stroke. As if there were a good time.

So, we'd all go to school during the day and go to the hospital to visit my rehabbing mom in the evenings. I wasn't seeing much significant progress, so you can imagine my surprise when about two weeks into her rehab stay, she reported that the social worker had visited with her that afternoon, and she was set to come home to my house when she was released.

"What?" I questioned her.

"I just talked with her this afternoon. I told her I'd be living with you when I got out."

"When do you think you'll get out?"

"Two weeks. At the end of March."

My mom seemed really sure about this.

I seemed really sure that there was no way in the whole wide world that she was ready to live at my house.

Brian and I both work full-time outside of the home. The girls would do anything for their Nana, but they were in no position to actually do these things for their Nana. My mother still required two people to get out of bed. She was incapable of getting herself to and from the bathroom without assistance. She could not dress herself, and she could barely move her wheelchair without assistance.

"What is the social worker's name?" I asked before I headed home for the evening to have a nervous breakdown.

The first call, since it was after hours, was to my sister. We both agreed that while it'd be ideal for our mom to be at my house, she didn't have the independence she'd need to live at my house.

The next call, first thing the next morning, was to the social worker.

This would be a good time to mention that just a few weeks before my mom's stroke, I had my yearly exam with my primary care physician. It was at this visit that he pronounced me in great health ... except for my blood pressure.

Apparently, I have white coat syndrome and my blood pressure likes to spike when I'm feeling nervous or anxious. And, apparently this is not a good thing. I thought it was okay because it wasn't high all the time, right? Wrong. But, with all this new fangled knowledge that my doc learned in med school, I ended up taking blood pressure medication. It was during this call to the social worker that I conceded that my doctor was probably right.

"Hi! I'm calling to talk about my mom," I started off, breathing deeply, hoping I didn't come across as frantic as I was feeling.

"Oh yeah. I thought you'd be calling," she said, I could hear my franticness echoed in her voice.

"Really? Why?"

"Well, I'm kinda new at this, and I shoulda called y'all and met with all of you at once."

"Um, yeah." I nodded my head in agreement even though she couldn't see me.

"And, I don't think your mom really understood what I was trying to say."

"What were you trying to say?"

"I was trying to say that she could go to your house?" She raised her voice a little bit at the end so that it sounded like a question.

I literally felt my blood pressure meds coursing through my veins. "What does her rehab team say about that?"

"Well," she sighed. "I haven't had a chance to meet with them."

It was then that the meds actually spoke to me and said, "We've talked to your heart, you're good for now."

The next week, my sister and I met with my mom and the social worker—who had visited with the team prior to our meeting—and we decided that, since she still qualified for more rehab time, we would move her to a rehab center until she stopped making progress.

"If you were at my house and there were a fire, could you get yourself out of bed?" I asked my mom.

"No," she admitted, "but you could help me."

"What if I'm not home?" I tried to keep my voice calm so that my mom could see where we were headed with the conversation.

"Someone will be home, right?"

"No, you'll have to be more independent before you come to our home."

She then channeled Amy Winehouse and said, "No, no, no."

Other Famous People My Mom Will Eventually Relate To

Maria Von Trapp—She will on more than one occasion refer to her therapists as Nazis; and as she learns to walk again, she will feel like she's climbing every mountain.

O.J. Simpson—With her afflicted right hand, she won't be able to make any glove fit.

Lady Gaga—When she is angry with my sister or me, she'll be sporting her Poker Face.

Lionel Ritchie—She'll complain that the staff at The Village is in her room *all night long* and that she can't sleep well, but the truth is that she'll learn to sleep through their comings and goings.

Drunk College Girls—when she rides around in the car for the first few times after her stroke, she'll puke her brains out. One time, she threw up in the sheriff's office parking lot.

Aunt Kay is Gorgeous

We convinced my mom that her coming to live with us was not out of the question, but she was in no position to be left alone during the day. She would have one hundred days of rehab, and we'd evaluate the situation at that time. It was spring break, and my sister and I spent the week looking at rehab facilities, which is a lovely way to spend a spring holiday.

(Could y'all hear the sarcasm in my voice?)

Aunt Kay and our cousin Courtney drove to Bartlesville from Dallas to offer moral support as we traveled from one center to another. Courtney, Kay and Rachel all took notes. I looked around and sniffed a lot.

(What do old people smell like? *Depends*.)

We had decided to look at places that were not only used for rehabilitation but were also used for long-term care as well just in case Mom didn't recover enough to come home.

As we traveled from one facility to another, Courtney, Rachel and Kay would compare notes—finances, meal planning, cable TV, roommates, private bathrooms, social activities. These were all things that you don't expect to discuss concerning a seventy-five year old woman. Some places didn't offer much information unless we asked the specific question and some places offered way too much information, and I left feeling overloaded.

The last place we went was The Village.

My sister and I were familiar with The Village. In 1999, when our dad had one of his strokes, he ended up in The Village for his rehab. That particular stroke was a true game-changer for my dad. With that stroke, he lost the use of both hands. He could still walk, but he wasn't stable on his feet. And his mind had changed. I walked into his room one evening just in time to hear him tell his roommate that the bitch who married his son had only married him for his money. I might have agreed with him if 1) my dad had any sons, and 2) his pretend son had any money. Since I was the only one married, I assumed he was talking about gold-diggin' me. P.S. Brian is a teacher—he's got no money.

My dad didn't understand why he was there, and often times he wanted to go home at two in the morning. The staff would call my mom, and she'd go put him back in bed. Because my mom's an amazing person, she retired and took him home to care for him. My mom's memories of The Village were not pleasant.

But, at the end of the day, that's where we decided to place her for rehab. There were several reasons for this.

The first was that it didn't smell.

The second was that she would have a private bathroom.

The third was that it was less than a mile from my house.

But, the major reason we placed her there was that the director thought that Aunt Kay was a hottie (which she is), and we knew that he'd give Mom good attention in order to get into Kay's ~~pants~~ good graces.

So, my mom was discharged from the hospital's rehab program and admitted to The Village at the end of the March, almost four weeks after her stroke.

Aunt Kay made my mom a wreath for her door. (I told her not to put RIP on the ribbons.) I bought her some new shirts to wear, and Rachel hung a calendar. And all of a sudden, with the calendar on her wall, my mom became Rainman with counting the days.

"My release date will be July the fourth. Independence Day. That's ninety-nine days from now. That's fourteen weeks or two thousand three hundred seventy-six days or one hundred fourty-two thousand, five hundred sixty minutes or 8.554e+12 microseconds."

"*If*," I'd emphasized that word, "you can become independently mobile, and you never ask to watch Wapner at four o'clock."

About ninety-one days later, we sat with the care team and formulated a plan for Mom's release. She could get herself from bed and into her wheelchair. She could walk with a hemi-walker, which is half of a standard walker. She could transfer herself onto the toilet and off again. She could mostly dress herself (assuming bras are optional). She could walk herself. She was independent enough to come to our home ... and that's what she did.

We Interrupt This Book

I would be remiss if I didn't stop here and thank Brian. How many of us have husbands who are willing to give up a spare room to have a mother-in-law move in? I know that my own daddy wouldn't do it. In fact, when *my* nana had a stroke, my mom wanted to bring her into our home and care for her, and my dad said no. His reasons were valid, and they decided together that it wasn't the best placement for her.

My Brian, though. What a guy. Seriously.

There has never once been a moment of apprehension over my mom's placement.

When I needed to be with my mom, he held down the home front.

When I needed to cry, he was my shoulder.

When I needed him to cook, he ordered out.

When I needed him to listen, he nodded his head at appropriate times while checking Facebook on his phone.

When I needed the TV hooked up, he called the satellite company. Y'all! He called the satellite company! And not only did he get my mom's TV hooked up, but he got our bill lowered. See why I love him?

Editor's note: I know this guy. He's a keeper.

There Will Be Helpful People

When you find yourself facing a life-changing event—whether it be marriage, a new child, death of a family member, moving, caring for a parent, changing hair stylists, whatever—you will find that there are lots of people who have survived the same change and have lots of helpful advice and words of wisdom to share.

Allow yourself to soak in their knowledge and to partake of their insight. As I like to say, there's no reason to reinvent the wheel. I'd venture to guess that at least ninety percent of the people who are aware of your situation will try to be helpful. At least this was what I found to be true when I would share with people that my mother was going to be moving in with my family once she was released from rehab.

I'd also venture to guess that at least eighty-five percent of the people will offer support in some way.

If you need me to check in on your mom when you run to Tulsa, just call.

I'm bringing you over a few freezer meals so you won't have to worry about cooking next week.

If you need an extra few thousand dollars to put tile down in your mom's room, let me give it to you.

Okay, no one said that last thing to us, but it would've been really cool and super nice if they had.

I found that more times than not, people were willing to do nice things for me and my family, including my mom. And for those people, I am grateful. I am grateful that people were there to offer advice, lend a hand, share their knowledge, just be and do whatever we needed at the time.

But, not everyone was helpful ... Which leads me to my next chapter ....

There Will Be Stupid People

Our smallish Oklahoma city (or large-ish Oklahoma town, depending on your perspective) was the corporate headquarters for a very prominent oil and gas company through the mid-90s. Then the company up and moved to Houston like all the other oil and gas companies and left our town a retiree's haven. We still have a large chunk of the company within our metro area, such as it is, but by and large, the retirees from this corporation comprise the majority of our citizens.

Because of this, our hometown boasts two large retirement compounds—COMPOUNDS, y'all!—three assisted living facilities (plus one within one of the retirement compounds), numerous long-term care facilities, several short-term care facilities, and a very large senior citizen's community center and service complex.

With all of these facilities, my sister and I set out to get more information about options for our mom. We were fairly certain that her living with one or the other of us was the route we would take, but we wanted to explore everything there was to explore before getting her set up.

Our first stop was at one of the large compounds. It was located less than a mile from my home. It offered transportation to the post office and Hellmart, which were both just right across the street. It was also adjacent to Taco Bell. My mom is not a Taco Bell aficionado, but I thought it would be a great distraction for the kids when we went to visit.

A few short weeks before my mom's stroke, my mom visited her lawyer and had her draw up legal papers, including a will, that outlined her wishes for after her life. My sister was named executor and given power of attorney over our mom. Apparently, this was my idea. Apparently, I said I wanted nothing to do with executing my mom's final wishes. Apparently, we had an entire conversation about this. I am not aware of this conversation, but it does seem like something I'd say. Plus, numbers confuse me and my sister has a business degree, so I'm not arguing with her decisions. I am, however, arguing with the fact that I actually had that conversation. And while we're on the subject: I also do not recall, back in 1998, that my mom was to have a colonoscopy. I remember with great detail the phone call from my sister that evening of my mom's colonoscopy in which she told me that I wasn't very nice leaving her to care not only for our mom, but our dad as well and that while Rachel would have appreciate my help during the day, she did not want my help at all at that point. I had no idea. None. No idea whatsoever. I'm not sure if this is part of my mom and sister's grand scheme to make me think I'm losing my mind or if I really block out conversations that I find unpleasant, like wills and colonoscopies. Either way, my sister was privy to my mom's financial situation, and I was not. I am not complaining, truly; I am just stating fact.

It does make me wonder, though, what else I've missed because of these supposed conversations my sister and mom are having with me...

But, that's neither here nor there.

Except for when we stopped in at the first retirement compound and were given the sales spiel (because, let's be honest, leasing a retirement apartment in our town is much akin to buying a used car).

When my sister and I had politely nodded and smiled at the sales guy sufficiently, I asked him to cut to the chase. How much would it cost my mom to get an assisted living apartment in their complex? He gave us a number, and I nodded my head in the affirmative. I then glanced at my sister who was shaking her head in the negative and immediately changed the direction of my bobbing head.

We went to an assisted living property. Their rental price was more in our mom's price range ... if all she did was sleep there. It was another gazillion dollars if she wanted cable and half a bajillion dollars if she wanted a phone. If she wanted meals with them in the dining room, it'd be thirty-two patrillion Euros, with an expected tip for the help. If she needed help with laundry or medicines or, say she'd fallen and she couldn't get up, that'd be a eleventy-gillion Pesos, payable in cash and prior to the need arising. I nodded my head in the affirmative. My sister rolled her eyes at me and shook her head in the negative.

The more we spoke to these residential offerings, the more we realized that my mom's plan of living with me and my family was really the best plan.

Our last stop, however, was at the senior citizen's super center just to get more information about the options my mom would have once she was released from rehab. I called and made an appointment with a woman I'll call Ditz. I was going to call her Dork, but my sister reminded me that she was more ditzy than dorky. (See why my mom picked her to be executor?)

Rachel and I walked into the senior center and asked to see Ditz. A very sweet receptionist showed us to an office that did not belong to Ditz as evidenced by the name on the door and on the desk, but we sat there anyway.

Soon enough, Ditz came into the office and sat down at the desk, which did not bear her name and said, "How may I help you?"

I introduced us and reminded her that I had made the appointment to talk about services that would benefit our mom.

"Oh yeah," Ditz said pretending to know what she was talking about. "Remind me the situation with your mom?"

"She suffered a stroke in March. She's currently in rehab and is set to be released in July. From the looks of things, she'll be living with me," I explained, "but we want to know what other services may be available to her."

"Oh," she nodded and frantically took notes on a notepad that did not have her initials on the top. "And what kind of services are you looking for?"

I half shrugged my shoulders and glanced at my sister. "I'm not really sure. We kinda need to know what services are available."

"Oh," she nodded and again frantically took notes. I'm not sure what she was writing, though, because we really hadn't said anything notable. "So, do you have any idea of what kind of information you are looking for?"

My eyebrows knit together, and I stared at Ditz. I wondered if we were speaking the same language.

"Tell us about home health care services," my sister interjected in what I understood to be English, her eyebrows mimicking mine.

"Home health care," Ditz answered slowly as she wrote the words down as if she didn't want to forget them when she looked up from the notepad. "Okay. Home health care. What about it?"

"Can you tell us about it?" I asked, restraining myself from screaming out *Ohmygoodnesssake! whattheholyhelliswrongwithyoulady??*

"Um. Well. There are many different companies that offer it."

"Okay. And what services do they offer?"

"OH!" she exclaimed seeming to come alive, "Lots of services." She nodded her head as if to affirm that she was certain they offered lots of services.

I sighed. My sister sighed. We were getting nowhere with Ditz. Over the course of the next few minutes as we asked Ditz questions about the various services that may or may not be available to our mom, she asked us just as many and frantically wrote down everything we said.

Finally, exasperated at the insanity of our in-service that we were providing for this industry "expert," I said spying the service brochures behind the desk, "Could you just give us some pamphlets, maybe, and I can call home health care directly?"

"Oh sure," Ditz said with a smile, "Let me go get them." Then she got up from the desk and left the office, the brochures still behind her desk.

My sister and I sat there and sat there and sat there. Finally, I walked behind the desk, grabbed the pamphlets that I thought would be helpful and my sister and I walked from the office, meeting Ditz in the hallway.

"Oh, there you are!" she exclaimed, empty-handed. "Did you get all the information you needed?"

"Um, yeah," I answered. "Just one more question. Do you work with Alzheimer's or dementia patients?"

"Yes, we do," she smiled.

I nodded my thanks, and we went back out of to the car.

My sister and I were confident that she was a dementia patient.

T- Minus One Week

Maybe it was selfish, but I needed a vacation with my family before my mom came to live with us. Between summer school (teaching it, not attending it) and softball and golf and ever'thing else in the whole wide world, we had exactly one week (five days) to get away. We planned a very elaborate road trip to start on Tuesday and find us back home on Saturday, just in time to move my mom in the next Wednesday.

The Tuesday of our departure was like any other Tuesday except that I was going to get to sleep in. Sleeping in is one of my most very favorite things to do in the world ever. So, imagine my disdain when my phone rang at 7:30. I may or may not have uttered some foul words. Some very foul words indeed.

"Mom fell." It was my sister.

"What happened?" I asked with a very groggy voice.

"All I know is that she fell from her chair and has a knot on her head."

"I'll go see how bad it is."

I threw back the covers, tossed on some clothes and headed to The Village.

It was bad. It was really bad. I'm sure it was exacerbated by the fact that, as a stroke patient, she was on blood thinners. The knot on her head? It was as if a cantaloupe had been lodged just above her eye.

And, she actually didn't fall from her chair. She was being pushed without her feet rests (foot rests? I have no idea about wheel chair terminology.), and her feet dropped to the floor essentially catapulting her from the chair. The good news is that she wasn't injured any place else. Just her forehead. And now her eyes. While I was standing beside her asking her questions, her eyes had blackened.

"Do you need to go to the hospital?" I asked my mom.

"Oh no," she said, lying through her teeth, "I'll be just fine."

I rolled my eyes then looked at the nurse, "Does she need to go to the hospital?"

The nurse shrugged her shoulders and muttered something akin to *Idunno*.

I went home and called my sister. "I don't know," I whined. "She says she's okay, but she looks really bad."

Ten minutes later, as we were pulling out of our driveway to start our much-needed and highly anticipated vacation, my sister called me. "Mom's going to the hospital. Apparently you got them to thinking that maybe she did need to be checked out."

And the first stop on our vacation was the Emergency Room.

eeeeeeeee

I met my mom in the triage room of the ER. Her eyes were almost completely swollen shut and her face looked as if someone had thrown a handful of black soot onto her face.

"How ya feeling?" I asked her.

"I'ng gud-h," she said through her swollen lips. I used my deduction skills and my prior knowledge to interpret her mumbling to mean *just fine*.

My sister met us just before they took my mom for a CT scan.

Almost two hours later, the ER doctor concluded that she had no internal injuries. As a precaution, they removed her from her blood thinners for a few days and made arrangements for her to return to The Village.

"Ill I til dit out nex eek?" she mumbled through her swollen pie hole.

"Yes," I confirmed. "You'll still get out next week. Until then, we're going on vacation."

Being The Ham In The Sandwich Generation

Cast Of Characters

My mom / Our Mom / Mom / The Stroke Patient: This part will be played by Harriett. She'll also be called Nana. Say it like this: Naw-Nuh. Or like this: Non-uh. Sometimes the girls get lazy and call her Non.

Brian, Hadley & Briley: If you've read any of my other books, you are already quite familiar with them. Hadley is formerly known as Daughter 1 and Briley as Daughter 2.

Rachel: She's my neurotic, but gets-things-done sister; she is married and has a really cute kid.

Aunt Kay: She's my mom's younger sister. My mom was twelve years old when Kay was born. Kay looks way younger than I do. I use Oil of Olay and Aunt Kay, well, I think she uses a professional.

Cousin Courtney: She is Aunt Kay's younger daughter. She has two really cute kids. She's also really good at asking the right questions at a senior residence facility and she's super good at cleaning out houses.

Cousin Whitney: She is Aunt Kay's older daughter. She has three boys. The boys and I follow each other on Instagram and that makes me feel really cool. Whitney doesn't do social media; she's kinda elderly that way.

Here We Go

We had our vacation and returned home relatively unscathed. It seems like we barely had our bags out of the van before we started moving furniture and making calls. Slowly but surely our formal dining room (which I lovingly referred to as my formal crap-collecting room) was transformed into my mom's room.

Brian tirelessly made trips to her house to bring back her TV and computer. We moved a desk and dresser into her room and added decorations. Handrails were added beside the toilet and the shower. Rachel and I spent some quality time picking out a toilet seat raiser. "Would the gray or white seat be better?" Y'all? It's a toilet seat. It doesn't matter.

Lie. This is a lie. It does matter. We picked the grey because it seemed less likely to show, um, ahem, ya know ... crap.

The satellite guy showed up to hook up my mom's television and to fix our DVR box. Then the company sent us another box ... and another box ... and another. And truthfully, it was the only trip up we had transitioning mom from rehab to ~~our crap-collecting room~~ ~~formal dining room~~ her new room at our house.

We were set. My sister had spoken with a home medical place and the bed would be delivered the same day Mom was released. I had spoken with the home health providers, and they made plans to visit on July 4. These home health care providers are hard core.

We sent a text or an email to those who needed to be in the know that Mom was ready to be paroled. We packed up most of her stuff from The Village the night before and brought it to her new room. The night before she broke out, I said goodbye to her and her empty room. Then I went home to sleep fast.

The next morning she called at 5:17 and asked where we were and why we weren't there to take her home.

I'm just kidding. She didn't really call that early. She called at 5:32.

Conveniently, Brian had a meeting all day on July 3, which Mom had taken to calling her own Independence Day. I left the girls at home, and Rachel met me at The Village. We collected her medicines, her nightgown (which was all she had left at The Village), pushed her on one last round to say her goodbyes and then took her home.

I had made arrangements with Mom's favorite food truck, Shortie's Grill, to have her favorite chicken salad sandwich ready for her lunch. We unloaded her and wheeled her into my house. We all breathed a little sigh of relief; she was home.

lllllllll

The first few days found us breathing little sighs of relief on a regular basis.

She was scheduled to have physical therapy ... whew. She still had a long way to go with her walking.

She was scheduled to have occupational therapy ... sigh. Her hand and arm movements were slow in returning.

She was scheduled to have a bath assistant ... *oh thank goodness*. Who wants to bathe her own mother, for heaven's sake? (This statement will eventually come back to bite me in my soon-to-be sopping wet toes.)

She had an at-home appointment with our friend Sheri to cut her hair ... Mom was looking kind of bushy since being on the inside.

She used the bathroom by herself without assistance. She got into the newly-delivered bed without assistance. She maneuvered her way through the house without assistance. I felt confident that this situation would work.

The next day, we grilled out to celebrate not only our nation's freedom, but my mom's freedom as well. We loaded her into the minivan and went out to enjoy the fireworks. From a rooftop. I wanted my wheelchair-bound mom to stay in the minivan, but she insisted on getting out. Brian sided with my mom. I would not be having sex with him for a while. I would have to think of a different thing to withhold from my mom for her defiance.

She got out of the van and into her wheel chair. Brian pushed her to the edge of the rooftop parking deck (literally not figuratively), so she could have a better view. I nearly peed my pants and had visions of Michael Jackson dangling his poor baby from the hotel balcony over the screaming Paris crowd.

Good news (which you probably already guessed since this isn't the end of the book): my mom did not fall over the edge of the rooftop. Hadley and Briley got into a little bit of a shoving match and nearly gave me a heart attack, but they were able to return home unscathed as well.

The rest of the weekend went slowly but easily. That was probably a good thing ... Because when Monday rolled around, well, let's just say that I considered going back to the rooftop and jumping myself.

Not really.

Heights make me nervous—just in case you couldn't tell.

All The People In The World

My immediate family is pretty standard. One mom, one dad, two kids, two dogs. I grew up in a very stereotypical family as well ... but we only had one dog at a time. And that was very worrisome to me because I felt like my sister and I should each have our own dogs. My dad, however, didn't want any dog at all, and my mom barely wanted one. My sister and I promised to take care of the dogs every single day, giving them water and food morning noon and night and walking them for a good three miles every day when we got home from school. Still, my parents stood firm and denied our having more than one dog, saying things like, "Get out there and play with that poor dog" and "If it weren't for me your dog would have no food or water all week" and "How can the leash be missing when you never use it?"

Now that I'm a mom, I get it. But, I'm a much slower-learner than my parents as we have two cats and two dogs—all of whom are neglected by their under-aged "owners" on any given day. But,

I'm okay with taking care of the livestock because I know in the end they love me best and really, that's what pet ownership is all about—having an animal that loves you best.

Wait. I know I wasn't talking about pets when I started this chapter ... give me a minute.

Oh yeah. Families. Okay, I'm back on track now.

My mom grew up in a much bigger family. She had one mom, one dad, two half brothers, two whole brothers and a baby sister. Her half brothers passed away before I was born, but her remaining three siblings each have two kids and they are married and have two (or more kids). Much. Bigger. Family. When we have our summer get-together or our Christmas gathering, and everyone shows up, there are forty-three of us, forty-four if my aunt's love life is in an upswing.

They did not all show up at my house the week after she was released, but it kinda felt like it—what with the medical visits and such. Add to this, the physical therapist who came by to do an evaluation so she could write up a therapy plan. There was the occupational therapist who came by to see what kind of set up my mom could use in her hand and arm therapy. There was the speech therapist who wanted to hear my mom breathe—I know. It was weird because this was never an issue before, but I didn't question it because hey! Free therapy! There was the bath assistant, um, excuse me, the personal care assistant who wanted to know exactly how much my mom was able to bathe and care for herself. There was the neighbor who wanted to make sure everything was all right. There was the passerby who wanted to know how my Little Free Library worked. ("So I just take a book and leave a book? When's it due? How do I check it out? Where's my little free library card?") And, there was the cop.

A cop? Yes, a cop. We'll get to him in a minute.

First, let me make it clear that I love my family. I adore my family. In fact, I would sometimes rather spend time with my family than I would my friends. (No offense to the friends who have bought this book.) We truly do have the best time together. I'm not just saying that to make them feel better either. I'm pretty sure that none of them are reading this book right now because they are still waiting on me to give them a copy. (Sorry, guys, I don't get free copies of my books—you aren't getting one from me unless you give me $12.99, plus shipping.) Except my cousin Courtney. She tells me that she buys my books. And she wants me to sign them. But now that I'm thinking about it, she's never actually let me sign one.

Curious ...

Anywho. The week after my mom came home, the house was bustling with activity. I fried some chicken, which is to say that I let my uncle Sam Walton (owner of Hellmart) fry the chicken. I made (read: bought) potato salad, coleslaw and baked beans. My aunt Kay and my aunt Liz brought desserts. My cousins Courtney and Whitney brought the bigger-than-life-sized barrel of cheese balls—it's their signature dish. (If my books were available at Sam's club, I know for a fact that they'd buy my books because they buy everything there.)

We had everyone at the house.

Except Aunt Kay's boyfriend, 2014.

(His name is not really 2014, but I got tired of trying to remember them all, so I just give them a number now.)

(Also, she hasn't had 2,014 boyfriends—I don't think—I just assign them a year, like a car. I used to actually call them "2009 model," but that joke wore itself out when the 2010 model became the 2011 model and we thought we were going to have to learn his actual name.)

(Also-also, the fact that 2014 was not there will be a very important fact for the next chapter. Right now, though, I'm trying to tell you about the cop. Sometimes, my mind is my own worst enemy.)

After dinner, the crowd thinned some, but all of the kids were still at the house, still wreaking havoc into our lives, still thinking that they were using their inside voices when, in fact, they were using their outside megaphone voices. And they were not outside. Nor were they using actual megaphones—just voices that sounded like megaphones. (Hadley would like it noted here that she was at summer camp when all this went down, so she wasn't a bother to anyone; instead, she feels forgotten and hurt that life went on without her.)

In our best parenting move to date, we rounded up enough electronics for them each to have one device in their hands and we shut them in a dark room and told them to stay out of our hair.

Not really. For the most part, the six kids really did play nicely together. The Texas twins—Brecken and Gavin—and their brother LJ got along famously with Briley, Bree and Bode. They were all athletes so their time together consisted of sportsy-type things and phrases like this: *Throw me that ball*, *Watch this*, and *You just got struck out by a girl*. (True story: My little pitcher-girl struck out the super-stud baseball players. In their defense, most baseball players can't hit off of softball pitchers. Also, girls rule.)

The two littles, my niece and Courtney's younger child, are the same age. They really did just want the electronic device. It was in their quest to try and listen to music ("All About That Bass" was their song of choice) and play Two Dots at the same time in which the incident happened.

The bigger kids were outside hitting cars with baseballs when the house got suddenly quiet. This should have been our first clue.

Our second clue should have been when Bode and my niece came running into the living room, their little preschool faces looking very somber.

"Um, I called the cops," my niece confessed.

"Yeah," Bode verified while pointing his little thumb to his cousin, "she called the cops."

We laughed. How cute was that? They were playing cops and robbers. It was refreshing to see young kids still using their imaginations and not just a screen. But their little four-year-old selves were trying to tell us something.

"I called the cops," she reiterated.

"She called the cops," Bode confirmed.

"Okay," we said back to them and pretty much continued on with our conversation. Slowly, they left the room.

Then my sister, who's always been a thinker and a glass half-empty kinda person popped up. "Were y'all playing with the phone?"

"I called the cops," my niece spoke plainly to her mother.

"Yeah," Bode continued to have his cousin's back in her confession time, "she called the cops."

Brrrrrriiiiinng! Brrrrriiiiinng!

At that point, when the phone began to ring from the other room, that all of the adults picked up on what the pre-school set was trying to tell us.

Brrrrrriiiiinng! Brrrrriiiiinng!

"BRING US THE PHONE!" we shouted in unison.

Brrrrrriiiiinng! Brrrrriiiiinng!

My niece scurried to the other room to retrieve the phone.

Brrrrrriiiiinng! Brrrrriiiiinng!

She raced back into all the adult eyes watching her and threw the phone at me.

Brrrrrriiiiinng! Brrrrriiiiinng!

I frantically tapped the screen, sliding my thumb over any slidable icon to receive the call. The caller ID indicated that it was an "Emergency number."

Brrrrrriiiiinng! Brrrrrriiiiinng!

"HELLO!??!?" I shouted bringing the phone to my ear and holding my breath. The entire room, minus the little athletes, followed suit.

"This is the Bartlesville Police Department. We've received several 9-1-1 hang up calls from this number."

I let out a nervous giggle. "Yeah, my niece and cousin, who are four-years-old, were playing with the phone."

"Tell them I wanted to listen to 'All About That Bass,' okay?" my niece interjected.

"But I wanted to play Two Dots," Bode inserted.

"So, there's no emergency?" dispatch answered, seemingly not caring that the two four-year-olds were having a sincere issue trying to figure out how to do both—so much of an issue that they locked the phone and made an emergency call.

"No unless you count some discontented preschoolers as an emergency." I laughed.

Silence. My attempt at levity was met with silence.

"No ma'am," I muttered. "No emergency."

"Do we need to send an officer by?" she responded.

"No unless one of the other kids knock a window out playing baseball."

Again, my humor was not appreciated as the dispatcher's end of the conversation turned silent.

"There's no emergency," I said in my best apologetic voice.

When I hung up the phone, Bode made one last statement to insure his innocence, "She called the cops."

"Yeah," I nodded my head, "I know."

You might think that a wise woman would've taken the phone away from them. But, alas; I am not a wise woman. I started the music and the game and sent the little cousins on their way.

The dispatcher, however, was a wise woman. A cop was situated at the end of our block all night. This was probably a preemptive strike.

Or maybe it was because they were running surveillance on a gun-running, drug ring.

Keep reading to find out more about that.

Kids And Their Relationships

Aunt Kay.
Seriously.
I love her.

She's only twenty years older than I am. I've already told you how gorgeous she is and how those good looks got my mom a great room at The Village. She's savvy in the ways of the world, the heart and the mind.

And, she's single.

I have a teenage daughter and a tweenage daughter. Neither one of them have the same social life that Aunt Kay does. (The tweenager will give Aunt Kay a run for her money in a few years, though.)

Aunt Kay, who lives in Texas, tries to come up every month or so to visit her only sister, my mom. She calls weekly and stays in touch. She answers our texts about meds. (She used to be a drug rep pimping out Viagra, so she knows things.) She encourages my mom and my sister and me. Throughout my mom's hospital stay, rehab and transition home, she's been nothing but supportive and reassuring.

Except when her boyfriend, the aforementioned 2014, calls. As was the case that lovely July day when all the people had come to see my mom. Just as we were getting ready to eat, 2014 calls. My aunt, trying to be polite, excuses herself and steps outside to visit. Her daughter, Courtney, stands at the front door and peeks out of the blinds, miming for her to hang up the phone and come back inside so we can eat. My aunt, who sometimes gives my tweenager a run for her money, mimed back for Courtney to shut up.

We went ahead and prepared for dinner, scooting my mom to the table and fixing the kids' plates, which they would eat in front of the TV—tell me I'm not mother of the year material.

Courtney went back to the front door to try and lovingly persuade (or shame) Kay into hanging up the phone and joining us for dinner. Kay had, however, moved.

We looked through the front windows and front door and couldn't find her. Courtney opened up the garage door and discovered Kay sitting on the hammock, twirling her hair, grinning and giggling as she talked to 2014. Courtney swears she heard her mother saying, "No, you hang up first. No, you..."

Seeing her chance to get her mom back for every embarrassing thing she had done through Courtney's teen years, Courtney hollers out, "Get off the phone right now, young lady, before I take it away from you."

Then, Courtney laughed.

I feel it necessary to explain to you right here and right now that Courtney has the best laugh in the whole wide world. She laughs with every molecule in her being. It's loud. It's proud. It's full, and it's infectious. So without even knowing exactly why Courtney was laughing, my mom, sister and I were laughing too.

In between our ha-has, we asked what was so funny. That's how infectious Courtney's laughter is.

Even though Courtney is the youngest cousin in our generation and is in pretty good shape, she has had two kids, so not only was she laughing, but her legs were crossed to keep from peeing, "Mom just fell!" she interjected between her hardy-har hars.

My sister and I continued to laugh but jumped from the table with our phones in our hands. Rachel, my sister, will tell you that she was prepared to call 9-1-1 (despite our sordid history with the emergency service) in case Aunt Kay needed assistance. I will admit that I grabbed my phone to take a picture.

My mom couldn't jump up, because, well, she's a recovering stroke patient. She just sat at the table and called out, "What? What's happening?" The kids? Well, they kept their eyes glued on whatever nonsense Nick Jr. was spurting at them.

I peeked over Courtney's shoulder to find my aunt, her phone still stuck to her ear, laying on the ground, her legs still tangled in the hammock.

"I told her to come in, and she stuck her tongue out at me," Courtney related through her guffaws. "Then the hammock flipped her out!"

I snapped a picture. My sister did too when she realized her intentions to call 9-1-1 were unfounded. My aunt? Well, she continued talking to 2014.

Sometimes being a part of the sandwich generation is not about care-giving—it's about guidance. Just ask Courtney ... once she stops laughing, that is.

Seniors and Socialist Media

Several years ago at a writing conference I took a session on Social Media. I felt pretty social media savvy, but I like staying informed. Plus, my friend Lela Davidson was teaching the class and I pretty much wanted to be her when I grew up, so I didn't hesitate one bit to walk into the session and sit right down at a back table.

Shortly after the session began, a sweet little octogenarian couple slipped in the door and sat down beside me. She flipped open her steno notebook and began writing in actual short hand. He opened his conference program and began slowly turning the page.

She shushed him and his page turning then she leaned over to me and said, "Is this the socialist media class?"

I sighed. I figured she had watched a little too much Fox News either at home while eating Meals on Wheels or waiting in the doctor's offices. (All doctor's offices show Fox News. It's their response to Obamacare.)

I nodded to her that it was the social media class. I started to correct her and explain that it wasn't socialist media but before I got a chance to delve into such beautiful things like Facebook and 140 characters and poking your friends she asked yet another question, "Do you think Lola will teach us how to Google?"

I couldn't resist. "Not in this class, but in the hotel bar after the closing session, she might teach you how to Dougie."

"Oh. Very good then," she nodded and wrote something in short hand. Her partner was asleep with the program book open across his chest.

Lela did an excellent job teaching us all how to Google and poke and whatnot. I didn't keep track of the older couple. I'm not sure if they showed up in the bar that night expecting Lola to teach them how to Dougie or not. But, that little exchange with them gave me the humor I needed to face my mom's return to Facebook after her stroke.

"Is my computer hooked up?" My mom asked on the first day she was out of rehab.

"Your bed is not even here yet," I answered trying to give her some perspective.

"I don't care," she answered back, "If you hook up my computer and get me on Facebook, I'll probably just stay up all night and not use the bed anyway."

I retorted, "Oh no you won't, old lady. When you come into my home, you will abide by my rules. I am the only one allowed to stay up all night on Facebook."

I didn't really say that; I just thought it would be funny.

What I did instead was sign my mom onto Facebook and let her check her "99+" notifications and her "99+" messages. She hadn't been on Facebook since March 1, after all. It was a wonder the Internet didn't crash down upon itself without her presence.

There was really only one problem as far as I could tell about my mom's social media presence: She had no use of her right hand.

Her mouse was still set up for a right hand user.

This presented a problem for my mom, the quintessential Facebook scroller.

We adjusted the mouse for her left hand, changing the clicker so she could use it with ease (sorta) with her left fingers. This should have corrected the problem, and I was certain that in no time at all, she'd be right back to sharing articles that should have been Snopes-checked and liking pages like "I F#@&ing Love Science" and then wondering who put the eff-word in her newsfeed.

But, the next day, as I sat in the living room posting links to Snopes on shared and fraudulent articles in my timeline that told of maggots found in Lunchables and people dying from eating Pop

Rocks while drinking Diet Coke, my mom called out to me.

"Heather? When you aren't busy, could you come help me?"

"With what, Mom?" I called back, "These pictures of Channing Tatum's baby aren't going to like themselves, you know."

"I can wait until you're finished, but I'm pretty sure my computer's broken."

A broken computer was not something I was ready to deal with. I set my Macbook off to the side and went to assist my mom.

"I have no idea what happened," she said pointing to her screen. "But it's just giving me the hourglass and it won't open up Facebook."

"How many times did you click Facebook?" I asked her incredulously as I looked at her screen.

"Only once," she lied, "Then all of this happened." She waved her left hand in front of the screen as if she were Vanna showing off the one hundred and seventy-six windows of Facebook that were open.

I shook my head. "You clicked more than once."

"No," she insisted, "Just once."

I pushed in her power button, feeling overwhelmed at the prospect of closing out one hundred and seventy-six windows to get back to her home screen.

"You're not supposed to turn off the computer that way," she proudly chastised me.

"You're not supposed to click on an icon one hundred and seventy-six times, either."

The good news is that she eventually got on Facebook again but only after being closely supervised.

ecececece

Within a week, she had opened up Gmail in ninety-two screens, lost her home screen, signed up for Twitter and accidently followed Kanye West, and tagged me in a photo that belonged to a man I had never seen of before.

"The problem is," she explained one night, "that my mouse doesn't work right. I click it once and it clicks fifty times."

"Mice don't do that, Mom."

"Well, my mouse does."

My sister came to her rescue and got her a new mouse. This mouse is the size of a large, swollen flask. The bright red mouse ball is the size of a golf ball. This new mouse has only allowed for Facebook to be opened thirty-seven times during a session. And I've only been tagged in one stray picture.

So, you know, progress.

Life Imitating The Written Word

For three years, I was the co-producer for the Oklahoma City Listen To Your Mother Show. If you don't know what I'm talking about, take a moment now to crawl out from underneath the rock you've been living under and Google it. I'll wait.

Pretty cool, huh?

In February, before my mom's stroke, we held auditions for the Oklahoma City Listen To Your Mother show. We heard about fifty amazing stories about moms and narrowing our cast down to a dozen stories that worked together was a daunting task, but Misti, Julie and I did it. This particular year's auditions were particularly heart-wrenching in that about half of them were about the loss of a mother or mother-figure. That evening as we set the cast, I joked that my piece would start off with the words, "My mother's not dead."

We laughed, drank some margaritas, went home and called our year's cast. The next day, I wrote my Listen To Your Mother piece called, "Risky Business" and it started off with "My mother's not dead ... yet."

The next week, my mom had her stroke. All of a sudden, my humorous piece became a sentimental piece. I confessed a thousand times to a thousand people that I wasn't sure how I could read my piece. But, when push came to shove, I knew I had to. And I did. My voice cracked during it because the funny parts could now be seen as prophetic. But, the audience laughed and saw the humor in the strange relationship that mothers and daughters have, so it worked well as a healing piece for me and a laughing piece for everyone else.

ℓℓℓℓℓℓℓℓ

Risky Business

My mom is not dead ... yet. But, she's been exhibiting some very risky behaviors, though. No, no, no ... she's not self-harmful, she's not using intravenous drugs or hitting the pipe, she's not sleeping around with strange men she's met at clubs ... in fact, I don't think there are any men, strange or otherwise in her women's group at church, and she's not taking the "Twerking for Grannies" class down at the senior center. But, she is clearly doing things that worry me.

Last month she told me of a strange van that was driving slowly through her neighborhood. She described the van as {quote} one of those big windowless kidnapper vans that people sometimes use for deliveries. {end quote} She just knew that this windowless kidnapper van was up to no good, so she followed it. She followed it, y'all. My mom was the Barney Fife of Oak Park Village.

"Mom!" I screeched, "That wasn't smart."

"Well," she explained, "I wanted to see what the perp was up to."

She went on to rationalize that it'd be hard for the driver of the van to commit any crimes with a member of the neighborhood watch committee on his tail. She did decide to turn it over to the police after about fifteen minutes of tailing the culprit. Fifteen Minutes.

She was a little bit miffed when dispatch (which is what she calls the people who answer the phone when she calls 9-1-1) told her that it was not illegal to drive around doing nothing. She was even more miffed when they told her that following another vehicle just for the sake of following him border-lined on stalking. Even if she is a 75-year-old member of the neighborhood watch committee. In her defense, she is pretty formidable when she stands in her front yard, shaking her cane at the neighborhood kids as they ride through her yard.

Then there was the time that her little dog Chrissy got out of the yard. Chrissy was, um … putting out vibes that she was single and ready to mingle, so my mom got into her trusty minivan— not to be confused with a big, windowless kidnapper van—tracked Chrissy down along with about ten neighborhood strays. She rolled down her window and whistled for Chrissy to come. But that Chrissy is a hussy, and she did not respond to my mom's whistle. So, my mom punched her door-open button and opened the back of her van.

In no time at all, my mom had the dog in the back of her van. It wasn't her dog and it wasn't just one dog, it was about six dogs and they were big and in her van.

"Mom!" I screeched, "Why would you open the door to let those dogs in?"

"Well," she explained, "I didn't whistle for all the others."

On another occasion, she told me of picking up hitchhikers who looked cold, of a road trip by herself to buy a jar (or twelve) of Amish jelly. And one late Saturday night she heard on the scanner of a high-speed chase in our small-ish town, got out of bed, and joined the pursuit "from a safe distance. Just in case."

Just in case what??!?!

Granted: She is an adult. She can take care of herself. But, she's a 75-year-old woman with an artificial knee who obviously needed looking after.

I was in the middle of explaining to her the dangers of allowing stray dogs and stray humans into her van when I was suddenly stopped short in my big *Just Say No* speech. Our journey had taken us from "Don't let my mom know what I've done" to "What has my mom done now?"

When I was four, I remember packing my bags to run away from home. My mom actually helped me pack. My plan was to sit on the curb and wait for the city bus to come by, and I'd just get on and go wherever those ten wheels would take me. Wait. Does a bus have ten wheels? I don't know because we didn't have buses in my neighborhood. I'm sure that played an important role in my mom's decision to let me sit out on the curb in front of our house waiting for hours. Or maybe just ten minutes.

Never once, through my years of run-away attempts, late-night bike rides and creative license about where I was on any given Saturday night did she say to me, "I hope you have a child just like you." I think that was by design. It became clear to me now that she had planned all along to play the part of worrisome individual that I had been up to this point.

But, in my defense, I hadn't been that bad of a kid—those four weeks in college when I dated a boy known only by his nickname, "Boner," not withstanding.

I had brought home my fair share of stray animals. I had chased after cute boys in their 1985 Fieros. I had thought of myself as indestructible, much in the same way my mother was thinking of herself now.

Maybe our roles were reversing. *Sigh*. I wasn't entirely comfortable with the level of worry that change brought with it.

I knew I couldn't be with her twenty-four hours a day, seven days a week. And when I reconciled myself with that thought, the voice in my head sounded a lot like ... my mother.

My mom and I? We were swapping positions. The roles were reversing.

Or maybe we are both strong-willed and independent women who came into our own at different times of our lives. I had spread my proverbial wings in my early twenties, and she in her sixties and seventies.

So, maybe I just needed to let her be. I needed to trust that as her daughter I'd done everything I could to prepare her for this world. But, just in case she wasn't quite ready, I was signing up for the "Twerking For Grannies" class just to keep an eye on her.

It's hard to let our moms go completely.

And it's never too late to learn how to shake what your momma gave ya.

Other Ways I Wasn't Such A Bad Kid

I could have actually gotten the rubber bands around Johnny M's wrists when I tried to fake arrest him at the school playground.

I could have left the street sign lying in the middle of the street when I knocked it over.

I could have written my name in the wet cement when my dad and I put the street sign back in its proper place on the corner.

I could have brought home every stray dog I found (about six of them) the night I brought home the lone pregnant stray.

I could have taken off my shirt and played football with the boys in the street like my sister did.

Like Mother, Like Daughter

My mom missed the Listen To Your Mother show that year. She hadn't been in a car in about twelve weeks, and we didn't think a three-hour car trip was the best way to ease her back into the real-world.

As soon as we busted her out, though, I showed her the YouTube video. Not much was said. There was some sniffling involved. And then she told me that I had a wild imagination and that half of those things didn't happen how I portrayed them. I told her she'd had a stroke and her brain was wacked out, then I pulled out some veggie straws from the pantry, and we ate them as we laughed about her being on the neighborhood watch team.

Then, one mild July morning, something woke me up. I wasn't sure what woke me up, so I got up and went to the bathroom, which is what I always do when I wake up. I had just lay back down when I heard it. *This is the Bartlesville Police Department. Come out with your hands up!*

"Brian," I whispered, "I think the police are outside."

He grunted back, "Okay."

This is the Bartlesville Police Department. Come out with your hands up!

"Brian," I hissed and shook him. "The cops are here!"

"Where?" he grumbled.

"Here!" I insisted. "Listen."

This is the Bartlesville Police Department. Come out with your hands up!

"What do you want me to do?" he asked, stretching himself out.

"Go see if they're here, while I check my scanner app."

"Why would they be here?" he mumbled as he was getting out of bed.

"I don't know, but they've woken me up!"

My phone said it was 5:42 a.m. when I turned on the scanner. Apparently, the authorities had taken to radio silence.

Brian crawled back in our bed. "They aren't here."

"Where are they?" I asked.

"I have no idea."

So, I did what I had to do to protect my family. I pulled on some shorts, put on my glasses and set out to find the cops and see what they were up to, interrupting my summer sleep.

"What are you doing?" my mom muttered as I walked past her room to the garage.

"I'm channeling you," I answered as I grabbed the keys and began my cruise through the neighborhood.

Two blocks over, I drove down that street. Almost every single homeowner was out on their front lawns in their robes, holding their cups of coffee, looking around, obviously dazed and confused. A few even had their hands in the air.

Our neighborhood essentially stopped with this block. Behind this particular street was an apartment complex and on the other side of the complex was an older section of our neighborhood. It was there that I found the SWAT team, holding battering rams, a big tank-like vehicle parked in front of a house that had its windows and doors completely busted out.

I continued driving down that street, back toward my own home, as if driving around in the neighborhood at six in the morning with bed head and glasses were the most normal thing in the world.

I returned home to find my mom and Hadley both awake.

"Holy cow, Mom!" Hadley hollered. "I've never seen you up this early unless someone's puking."

"Your mother," my mom took great excitement in saying, "was out chasing the police."

"I had to protect my family, Moooom," I fired back in my best teenage angst voice.

"You are just like your mother," she shot back at me.

And maybe, I was. But, as far as I was concerned I was just being an involved citizen. And maybe— just maybe—I would wind up as the president of the Neighborhood Watch Program. I already had the scanner app, so I was good to go.

Okay, okay ... I know you are wondering exactly what happened to cause a no-knock warrant to be served at five in the morning. I wondered that myself and that's why I took off looking for it. Inquiring minds want to know, right?

Well, the weird thing about no-knock warrants is that they are kept kinda secret. And even though I politely asked the nice policeman holding a big weapon what was going on as I drove by that morning, he just wouldn't answer.

I texted my friend Deborah, who works with law enforcement and told her what had happened. I hoped that she would have texted back and given me the four-one-one. She did text back but didn't give me any information. In fact, she told me to keep her informed. Pfftt ... wasn't that *her* job in our relationship?

I did check-in on Facebook that morning as I drove by. My status was something along the lines of "I love the smell of police invasions in the morning." Within an hour, a friend of mine who lives two states away, sent me a link stating that the police had invaded a home and recovered drugs and weapons after a months-long investigation.

Thanks to social media, I've discovered that I'm a mighty fine detective.

I used my brilliant deduction skills to deduce that the cop who stationed himself by our house earlier in the summer was probably part of this sting operation. Because it certainly couldn't have been me they were staking out, right?

Hoarding Is Real, Y'all

My mom will tell ya that she's not a hoarder, which is something a hoarder would say. She will say that her house is nothing like the people on the show *Hoarders*. I will then remind her that the show is *Extreme Hoarders*. And she will admit to being a collector. Sure she is. She is a collector who had collected three of the same John Grisham book and over thirty-three pairs of scissors.

True story: The night before she had her stroke, Hadley and I were at my mom's house. Hadley asked for a pair of scissors. We couldn't find one single pair. When my sister and I started cleaning out my mom's house, we found over thirty-three pairs in boxes, in drawers, in bathroom cabinets.

But, she's not a hoarder.

One might say that this doesn't sound as much like she's a hoarder as it does someone who misplaces everything. (A loser?) But let me tell you one more thing: *thirty-three* pairs of scissors.

My mom told my sister and me that we lacked sentimentality; we had no respect for the things that really mattered, the things that made us who we are, the things that were our heritage, like scissors.

We very gently and respectully told her that she had a bunch of crap she needed to get rid of.

Once my mom was placed in the hospital's rehab program, my sister and I spent a large part of our time cleaning out her house. We got rid of the perishable (and already-perished) foods. We ditched anything that was broken or no longer useful. Then we started packing up the duplicates and preparing for a yard sale.

My sister and I collected boxes and boxes and boxes of things that were doubles or triples or quadruples. My cousin Courtney came up and we went through the garage together getting rid of things she either hadn't ever used or hadn't used since Reagan was in office. Finally, with her house half full of boxes, we set a date for the garage sale.

Rachel borrowed tables from her church—ten, eight-foot long tables to be exact. My mom had four crafting tables and one card table.

Briley had a softball game on garage sale day, so Hadley and I met Rachel at my mom's house, and we began unpacking the boxes and setting things out to sell. I advertised on Facebook and we sat back to watch our mom's house clean itself out. We filled every single table that was set out in our mom's driveway and front yard. We piled stuff on her tables and the sidewalk. We even dragged a shelf from her front room to put more stuff on. The stuff? It was all on display. All of the stuff in all of the world seemed to be in front of my mom's house.

The first shopper stopped by. She picked up a set of placemats. "How much?" she asked.

I shrugged my shoulders and looked at my sister, who shrugged her shoulders and looked me. Guess what? We hadn't priced anything that we had set out for sale. Not one thing had one single price tag on it—except for the vinyl table cloths (all eight of them) that she bought when the T G & Y store went out of business is 1983.

"What do you want to pay?" I answered back with a question of my own.

"A dollar?" she offered.

"Sold!"

And that's pretty much how the day went.

"I don't see a price tag."

"Pay what you want to."

"How much?"

"How ever much you want to pay."

We stayed busy, not overwhelmed, but busy. We sold stuff to people by the box-full. We made a lot of money for my mom and it seems that we sold a lot of her stuff.

At the end of the day, though, we packed up ten tables full of stuff to be donated. Oddly enough, the stuff seemed to reproduce when left out in the sun. Maybe she wasn't a hoarder after all. Maybe her stuff just multiplied. Nonetheless, we felt really accomplished, like we had made a dent in getting my mom's house under control and ready to be sold. Forty-three years of life packed into one home takes a lot to rein in. But this garage sale was a good start.

We were tired, but feeling confident in our efforts.

Then we walked back into the house. It didn't look like we'd made much of a dent at all.

My sister has clearly done the lion's share as far as our childhood home is concerned. Since my mom has been at home, she and Rachel have gone to her house regularly to clean it out and pack it up. This is how I came to host the second garage sale.

Since the "Name Your Own Price" strategy worked so well the first time, I gave it a go for the second one. But first, I had some ground rules.

At every garage sale that I or my friends and I had ever hosted, my mom bought stuff. Once she bought a figurine I had for sale because it looked sad to be leaving my house.

Once, she gave me a paper towel holder that I didn't want. I sold it in a garage sale and my mom bought it back. Two weeks later, she gave it to me yet again. This was a vicious cycle that my mom had going on. So, my first rule was that she couldn't *buy* anything. Not one thing. Nothing at all. Even if it looked really sad to be sitting out on a table being looked at by people with fanny packs full of singles, she could not buy it back.

My next rule was that she couldn't *take* anything back. As in the case of the paper towel holder. When I originally had it in my garage sale, she told me that she wanted it. Let's look at the extended paper towel holder saga:

"You already have a paper towel holder, but you can just have it back—you gave it to me," I reminded her.

"No, no, no. I couldn't do that, I'll buy it."

"Mom," I sighed, "You gave it to me. If you want it you can have it."

"Oh, I'll buy it." Then she gave me five dollars, and I tried to give her cold hard cash back to her. She refused, but she did take a couple of the kitchen gadgets I had for sale to make up for her having to buy back a paper towel holder. Guess what? She gave me the kitchen gadgets.

My final rule was that whatever didn't sell would immediately be donated. As in immediately, if not sooner.

My mom agreed to all of those things, and we set a date. We collected tables yet again—only eight this time—put everything out and announced that we were open. My mom made a lot of money that day. Since my sister had packed up most of the stuff we were selling that day, I actually turned into my mother.

I took back some embroidered towels that my grandmother had made. (My sister completely lacks sentimentality when it comes to those things.)

I also took back some Grimace mugs that McGaggles sold for fifty-eight cents when my sister and I were just six and ten. These are part of our heritage! My sister said she didn't want them, but I took them back anyway. (And then I marked her name off my Christmas shopping list. Merry Christmas, sister!)

And I took back a green chip and dip bowl set. I love chips and dip. I love green glass, so I kept it because it really spoke to who I was. I took the green bowel set into my kitchen and set it on the cabinet.

The rest of that crap got donated without a second thought.

Because, you know, I'm not a hoarder either.

Words My Mother Uses Instead Of Hoarder

Collector
Vintage Aficionado
Gatherer
Amasser
Enthusiast
Gleaner
Accumulator
Saver
Investor
Buff
Appreciator

Actual Conversation Between
My Mom and Me
Two Weeks After The Garage
Sale

Me: Could you hand me those napkins over there by the green bowl set?

My Mom: I used to have a green bowl set like this.

Me: (snickering) Really? Just like that?

My Mom: Yes, I believe so. If we run across it at the house, I'll give it to you. I know that you like green glass.

Me: Are you serious?

My Mom: Yes. Where'd you get this?

Me: At your garage sale two weeks ago.

My Mom: Oh. No wonder I like it so well.

Is There A Patient In The House?

A little known fact about my mom: She was almost a doctor. Just ask her—she'll tell you. All she lacked was a college degree, medical school, an internship, rotations and graduation. Other than that, she could've been a doctor. She had read every single edition of *Good Housekeeping* and *Women's Circle* or whatever, so she pretty much knew as much as any doctor.

Just ask her—she'll tell you.

Prior to my mom's stroke, she went through a series of doctors after her long-time doctor retired and left town. The first doctor she saw died. The next doctor she tried to see was never in her office, and the third doctor she saw, well, she never saw— she either saw the nurse practitioner or the physician's assistant.

With each medical professional that she encountered, she pretty much dictated her care.

"Mrs. Smith, you have diabetes. I'd like to prescribe you some oral meds for that."

"Pffft ... I can control it with diet and exercise. Biscuits and gravy are good for diabetics, right?"

"Mrs. Smith, you have high cholesterol. I'd like to prescribe you some oral meds for that."

"I read on a friend of a friend's Facebook wall that those meds make you trip and fall, so no thanks."

(I can't imagine why she had a stroke.)

I talked long and hard to convince her and my sister that she needed to change to mine and Brian's doctor. I called his office and they would take her. In fact, he made calls to The Village, so while she was in rehab, he would actually be her doctor in the interim as well.

My OB-GYN recommended my primary care doctor to me when I was complaining that it was so hard to get into see my OB-GYN.

"But, you're not pregnant," he complained.

"I know—good job on that IUD, man."

He smirked, "And it's not time for your annual check up."

"But, I've got a really bad cold. My guess is that it's a sinus infection, and antibiotics are only available to me with a prescription," I explained.

"So go to your primary care physician," he uttered as he wrote out my prescription.

"You are now my primary care physician," I proudly announced right before he kicked me out of his office and handed me the business card for a very nice Internal Medicine doctor (and one for a psychiatrist, but that's neither here nor there).

I was very excited when my new primary care physician agreed to see my mom and got her medications all straightened out. He was very kind and concerned and treated her compassionately and respectfully.

When her discharge date was approaching, we called the office to arrange her first in-office visit with the doctor. Once all the family had come and gone, the police had come and gone, and home health care had come and been scheduled, it was time for us to go to the doctor's appointment.

You read that right: Us.

Mom's appointment was on a Thursday afternoon. We left the three grandkids with Brian while my sister and I took my mom into the doctor. You've got to admire a man who willingly walks into a room with three females and offers his help.

"Remember we want him to look at your toes. It might be gout."

"We should ask him about your bladder."

"I wonder how often he needs me take my blood pressure."

"And your blood sugar."

"And your pulse."

"We need to show him your brace."

"Don't forget we need to ask him about moving this medicine to night and that medicine to the morning."

"Fish oil!"

"Lipitor!"

"Physical Therapy!"

"Rah! Rah! Rah!"

This conversation went on for the fifteen minutes we waited for him to come into our room. I mean my mom's room—it wasn't really *our* room, right?

He knocked on the door and came into our room.

"Hello, Mrs. Smith and ... others,"

"Hello, Doctor," we said in unison.

No we really didn't. That would've been creepy and completely bizarre. (And now I totally want to do that!)

We took our time and told him of our concerns, asked our questions and eventually, we let him do his job and examine our mom.

We stopped answering questions for my mom when he had the nurse standing in the corner giving us the stink eye while wielding a syringe full of what I can only imagine was the strongest tranquilizer known to man.

He renewed the prescriptions he wanted Mom to continue and adjusted some others that needed changing. He signed our paper, requested an appointment in three months and went on his merry way.

The next appointment was set for a day after I was in school. "I won't be able to come," I told my sister. She scratched her head and knit her eyebrows together.

"Do we need to have an entourage when she comes in?" the receptionist asked.

We nodded our heads in unison and agreement ... But, she did have a point.

I can only imagine that the second appointment was not nearly as thorough or enjoyable without me there.

File This Under Things I'm Responsible For

Actual sign in the doctor's office:

Patients are now limited to one family member or support-team member in the examination room at a time.
Thank you for your understanding.

We're looking at you,
Heather Davis

Just Call Me The Pharmacist

When Mom was discharged from The Village, we were given a week's supply of her medications and a handwritten list of when each was given and what dosage. I carefully sat down, sorted through her pills and put together a week's supply of her daily medicines. She took meds at breakfast, mid-morning, noon, mid-afternoon, evening and at night. And should she happen to get up in the middle of the night or very early morning, there was a pill she could take at that time as well.

Right?

Who has time for that?

I mean, I know that the meds are really important, or we wouldn't be signing over a little piece of our souls when we pick up her refills. Surely there would be a way to uncomplicated her schedule since, ya know, to ensure she takes her meds at the exact right time there wouldn't be a medi-tech popping in. Medi-tech? Med-tech? Either way, we wouldn't have one.)

First, I called Aunt Kay. "Can Mom take this little pink pill at night? Would it really change anything? And can we move the giant grey pill to the morning?"

She gave me some advice and I did some mixing up of the ol' medicines.

Next, I called the pharmacist. "If my mom takes this ivory, oval pill at noon instead of at 2:30, what's the worst that could happen? And will the fish oil first thing in the morning cause any significant damage or totally offensive fish breath?"

Then, I called my friend Jennifer who recommended putting the fish oil in the freezer to keep the fish breath at bay. (Who knew? Jennfier knew.)

I shuffled the dosages around yet again and eliminated one of the awkward times.

Finally, I called the doctor's office and requested to visit with the nurse.

"I've just got to find a place for these last two pills so that my mom is taking pills morning, noon and night and not every two hours. Help a girl out, won't ya?" I whined. I felt close to tears at the accomplishment of taking a nine-times-a-day medicine schedule and cutting it by two-thirds.

Oh, my gosh! I had just created my own real life algebra problem. Who knew?

If a pharmacy opens at nine and three scripts are filled by twelve and two pills can only be taken with a mixture of prune-cherry juice and one script is a sleeping pill, do I have to wake the patient to board the six p.m. bus heading east at sixty-five miles an hour or is x an unknown variable sold by Pfizer for a total of $267 for a six week supply times two to the nth power?

Algebra—*shudder.*

Five minutes later, I had filled my mom's weekly pill keepers and gotten her meds down to only three times a day. I felt like I could be an algebra professor. No. Scratch that. I felt like I could become an air traffic controller easily enough after shuffling all of my mom's pills.

Don't worry, I don't really know what they do, so I can't write a pretend word problem for that.

About seven days later, my mom informed me that she needed her medicine box refilled. I grabbed her medicine bag and sat down with the pill dispenser feeling confident and cocky.

It was then that I realized I had not written down the new dosages and times. Dang it.

So close to being super woman and yet so far.

Poop

When one has a stroke, one expects to have some paralysis—possibly, hopefully, temporary. There may be some speech issues, swallowing issues, breathing issues, memory issues. It's possible that memory can be affected. (Wait ... did I already say that?)

But the thing that no one ever tells you about is the way a stroke patient's bladder and bowels are affected.

My dad, who ended up having several strokes over the course of his lifetime, had bladder issues with his last stroke.

My mom, who had her first major health issue at age 75 with her stroke, had both her bladder and bowel struck dumb by her stroke.

I didn't think this would be too much of an issue when she moved in with us. I think this is because I am naïve and stupid. I also hoped that if she did have an accident, she'd have it while one of her therapists was here. Or, better yet! She could have an accident while her shower/bath aide was here! Wouldn't that be convenient? It totally would be convenient! Therefore, it would never, ever, ever happen ... with me.

But alas, it did.

When a seventy-five year old woman didn't move fast before half of her body was paralyzed, she certainly doesn't gain any speed post stroke. And when Nature called to her, she did her best, she really did, but sometimes that didn't cut the cheese. Well, technically, my mom cut the cheese no problem on that fateful Saturday when no therapists were scheduled to show up ...

I kinda knew something was up when the plug-in air fresheners unplugged themselves from the wall and actually panted, but what gave it away was my mom's tell-tale whistle.

For as long as I can remember, my mom has used her signature whistle to summon me. When I was the next block over playing with my best friend, Bobbi, I knew it was time to come home when I heard my mom's shrill *Wheet Whoo! Wheet-o, Wheet-O, Wheet Whoo!* (That sounds like a whistle in your head, right?)

When my sister was down the street playing football with the boys (she was skins, by the way), she'd pull on her shirt and run home when the powerful *Wheet Whoo! Wheet-o, Wheet-O, Wheet Whoo!* made its way to her ears.

If we were lost in a department store shopping: *Wheet Whoo! Wheet-o, Wheet-O, Wheet Whoo!*

If it were time to leave Six Flags, the potent *Wheet Whoo! Wheet-o, Wheet-O, Wheet Whoo!* could be heard from the top of the Texas Giant.

So, needless to say, when my mom did not make it to the bathroom in time and her bowels exploded and then the content of her bowels made their way to every last bit of surface from her waist down, the commanding *Wheet Whoo! Wheet-o, Wheet-O, Wheet Whoo!* summoned me to the bathroom.

On that fateful day just a few short weeks after my mom moved in, we were going to have to take a shower ... on our own.

I'll spare you (most) of the gory details, but let's just suffice it to say that getting my mom onto the shower chair and under the shower stream. Involved a lot of shitty shuffling. This is not an expletive. This is the literal truth.

Actually, we have a permanent showerhead and also a removable shower nozzle just for occasions like that.

Actually ... No. Never in our wildest dreams (or, ahem, fantasies) is this anything we had imagined when we remodeled our bathroom and selected a high-end removable shower nozzle for our bathroom. That was not the thought behind that decision at all.

But it worked.

And since you brought it up:

Since Mom has come to live with us, I'm pretty certain—and I only speak for myself and not my beloved—that the intended use for the shower nozzle will never be realized again. Just sayin'.

But anywho, back to my story, Mom and I finally got her finagled into the shower and got the nozzle turned on. I handed it to her and handed her a rag, and handed her some shampoo and body soap and told her to get busy.

"This is going to sound weird, Heather," she managed to say with the shower nozzle spraying all over the bathroom and adjacent dressing room, "but I haven't given myself a shower or washed myself—other than my hands and face—since March 1. You're going to have to help me."

Another funny thing about strokes: You may not know what you've forgotten or what skills you are lacking until you cannot summon the thoughts to make yourself do them.

So, forty-two minutes (I timed it) and all the towels in my cabinet, including the hand towels, later, my mom was clean from her salt and pepper grey hair to her not-so-tiny, curled-under toes.

Together we dried off (yes, I had to dry off too), powdered up, smeared on deodorant and got dressed. Then we got the shoes back on, including her leg brace, dried her hair and declared the shower officially done—sixty-one minutes after we started it.

Sure, we wouldn't be going to the Olympics for showering any time soon; we'd have to work on our speed and efficiency, but we had conquered our first shower.

"Next time, I'll do more to help. It's coming back to me."

"I know, Mom. I know."

꙳꙳꙳꙳꙳꙳꙳

In case you are wondering, I normally have about fifteen towels in my cabinet. When Mom came home, I told my sister that I wanted more towels from Mom's house and she packed up a large—very, very large—moving box full of Mom's towels. I now have about thirty or so towels in that bathroom cabinet and about a hundred, million, bazillion hand towels in another bathroom cabinet because my sister thinks she's funny.

On this day, however, I silently thanked her for bringing them to me as we used them all.

Poop, Number 2*

*See what I did there? I made a punny—
poop is number 2!*

*Really, the more I think about it, this chapter
should be about showers, not necessarily poop—
although many of the showers were brought about
by poop, and the Poop, Number 2 title is really
catchy. I think I'll have to flush** it and start over.*

***It took me a lot longer to come up with that
pun. I probably need to get up and stretch my legs
before I start this next chapter.*

*Whew, I feel much better. Ready to start this next
chapter? Me too.*

April Showers Bring May Flowers. July Showers Bring Messes

It wasn't long after that first shower that my mom would come to need a second shower. And a third shower ... then a fourth. And none of these accidents occurred while a therapist was here. They all occurred on a weekend when I was actually home. Lucky me.

When Mom first came home, we were cautioned by the nurses, the doctors, the therapists, my aunt Kay, the lady standing behind me in line at Hellmart, the gentleman who walks through our neighborhood with a pooper scooper but no dog—all of these people and more said to my sister and me a thousand times over to make our mom do most stuff for herself. Much to my mom's frustration, we did.

In fact, well-meaning friends, therapist and my aunt Kay would ask Mom, "Are your girls letting you do things for yourself?"

(I liked the word letting—it implied that we were doing her a favor instead of being the lazy slave drivers that my mom was beginning to think of us as.)

"Oh yes," Mom would reply. "They won't do anything for me at all."

This was not entirely true, but close enough. It was a badge I wore proudly. It was a literal badge my mom wanted to pin to my back in the form of a "kick me" sign.

The second shower was not unlike the first shower. In exasperation, I sighed, estimating that it would take two hours, three loads of laundry and a claim against our flood insurance to bathe her.

Finally, after a very, very, very long time, I got her onto the shower chair and handed her a rag, soap, shampoo, bottle of Lysol. With her right hand lying useless next to her on the shower chair, she fumbled with all the bath supplies with her left hand.

"May usually gives me the actual shower," Mom explained, which was akin to saying *nanny, nanny boo boo.*

"May's a trained professional," I counted back. "But if you need a five-thousand word essay written, I'm your gal."

May was mom's personal care therapist. She gave mom a shower during the week and helped her do the personal care things that the rest of us breeze through in our morning and evening routines.

The third shower was only slightly faster because I had settled into a routine. We still used all of the towels, but we were using them more quickly and keeping the water contained to the bathroom and not the dressing room. Also? I didn't even get my hair wet. This was certainly an improvement.

With each shower, we became more and more proficient in what we were doing. We cut our time to just under an hour and we were only using two-dozen towels to contain the water to the bathroom.

Then, tragedy struck: May announced that her time with Mom was done. I wailed and beat myself with a wet towel, crying lamentations in vain. May kicked at me and ran for her car.

Without May, this meant that we'd have to do showers during the week—prior to this, our shower time had been limited to the weekends.

I threw a shower scrunchie at the back of May's car as she drove away. It only landed eight inches in front of me—those things make really bad projectiles—but I think my point was made. Even though, I'm not sure what my point was exactly.

I told Brian that I felt like a tweaker who's dealer had just cut him off. I was going to have to go all Walter White and start cooking my own meth.

Brian said I was being overly dramatic and meth had nothing to do with a shower. I threw the shower scrunchie at him, too.

Eventually, I sucked it up and decided to get a handle on mine and my mom's showering skills.

"Our goal today," I announced on Thursday night, "is to shower in under forty-five minutes and to use no more than six towels. Do you think you can do this, soldier?"

She asked if it would be awkward for Brian to start helping her because I was starting to scare her.

But, for that shower, we did it.

The next shower, I set our time lower. "Let's do this thing with only three towels and less than fifteen minutes."

"It takes me longer than fifteen minutes to get undressed by myself."

She was such a sour puss.

We kept trying and trying and trying to streamline the showering process. And it worked. We didn't need May! We had this thing down! I finally felt confident enough to let Mom have a go at it by herself, with me sitting just outside the bathroom in case something went down. Like her.

We got her on the shower chair, the nozzle in her lap (which was kinda, sorta how we originally intended for it to be used, kinda, but that's not the point here) and I yelled, "Go!" as I started the timer. She wasn't particularly fond of that part of our shower routine. I closed the door slightly to give her some *much*-delayed privacy. Twelve minutes later, she was done. Fifteen minutes later, she was dressed. Twenty minutes later, her hair was dried, her teeth were brushed, her skin was both powdered and moisturized and she was wheeling herself back to her room. Bam!

We had done it! We only used one towel, one hand towel and two washrags!

I felt like celebrating, but Brian wouldn't take me down to the courthouse so I could run up and down the stairs singing "Gonna Fly Now" *a la* Rocky. Really, he's such a killjoy. I once again threw the shower scrunchie at him.

"Get Away From Me!"

I started prepping for Mom to come home weeks in advance by front-loading vitamins. Brian and I are both teachers, which is to say that we are exposed to some of the most potent viruses known to man. Our immune system, after twenty years in the educational field, is built up and fairly strong, save for that one time a year when our tired bodies succumb to whatever the annual bug is for that specific year. This usually occurs right before or after a scheduled school break.

With Mom coming home, though, I wanted to be extra strong because there would only be one thing worse than bringing a virus home to her and that would be getting stuck with the virus myself with my mom at my home.

Regardless of her need for the wheel chair and her inability to use her right hand/arm at all, she is still a momma. If one of us got sick, she would be right there in the middle of it, trying to be a momma and take care of us. Quite frankly, that was the last place she would need to be.

Unfortunately, one late October night, I woke up feeling not quite right. My first thought was that someone was about to get sick. I checked on Mom, the girls and Brian, the dogs, the cats—all the living beings under our roof were just fine. So, I went to the bathroom and that's when I understood why I wasn't feeling quite right.

Between heaves, I hollered out for Brian.

"Bring me a rag!" *Heave*

"Find the Lysol!" *Blech*

"I think I'm dying!" *Puke*

At three in the morning, I put in for a sub. I slathered Phenergan all over my body, placed a cold rag over my face and chanted, "No more vomit ... no more vomit" endlessly. It worked. I woke up in two hours not throwing up, thank goodness. But the virus had changed direction and was coming out my back door.

(Isn't it weird that I had no problem writing vomit, puke and throw up, but went all metaphorical to avoid writing diarrhea? Maybe it's because it's so hard to spell. I'm sure that's it.)

It was almost time for the girls to leave for school. Brian took control of the morning activities and got them up and out. My mom, however, was another story. He had gotten her up, and she had gotten herself ready. Brian got the cereal out for her breakfast and the day had started while I lay in my bed chanting, "No more diarrhea ... no more diarrhea."

The house was quiet as was my tummy when I heard a small voice, "I'll bring you some crackers and soda."

The tell-tale rolling of the rubber wheelchair wheels told me that it was my mother.

"NO!" I hollered. "I can't deal if you get a stomach virus!"

"I'll be fine," she called back the wheels still squeaking down our tiled hallway.

"DO NOT!" I hollered, raising myself in bed too fast and then swallowing back the nausea.

"Let me help you," she pleaded.

"YOU WILL HELP ME BY GETTING BACK, SITTING BY AN OPEN WINDOW, AND GARGLING WITH LYSOL!"

"No, silly. I'll be fine." And the squeaking of the tires continued toward me.

I forced myself to move to the doorway and plastered a fake smile on my face. "See? I'm just fine. Go to your room and don't come out until I can stand on my own without leaning against the wall."

"Well," she conceded, "if you're sure you're okay."

"I'm fine," I half grinned. "See? I'm moving to the recliner so I can watch *The View*."

Leaning against the wall, I made my way to the recliner, clicked on the TV and settled into a coma with a wet wash rag over my mouth. Nodding my head and forcing a smile when I heard my mother's voice, I kept her at bay and away from the sicky germs I was envisioning permeating from my chilled skin.

The good news is that no one else got sick from my short-lived bug. The not-so-good news is that I essentially did not get my guaranteed day of rest that accompanies an all-night puke and poop fest.

But, that's the sacrifice I'll make to keep my family on the well side of health.

Not really. I missed my sleep.

Pulling Her Fair Share

Pre-Stroke, my mom had one major hobby: Shopping at Hellmart. In fact, we're certain that after March 2, their stock dropped significantly because she was not there to keep them in business. Coupled with her (not) hoarding problem, we weren't really excited to take her spending anytime soon. But, lest you think we totally left her out of the Hellmart arena, my sister and I would always ask her if she needed or wanted anything when we made our shopping runs.

One afternoon as I was loading my shopping list and my reusable shopping bags, I asked Mom if she needed or wanted anything. Her usual answer was no, so I was surprised when she nodded affirmative and then said she'd like me to get a dust mop.

"I have a broom," I told her, stepping into the garage looking in vain for the missing cleaning tool. "Somewhere," I added.

"Yes, but I want a dust mop. It does a better job than a broom, and it would be easier for me to use."

Who was I to argue with a woman who wanted to clean my house.

So, I got her a dust mop.

And a duster.

Also, I got her a new toilet cleaning brush. If she were going to clean, she might as well really clean.

Then, I made mention that if she were going to be dusting and sweeping and cleaning, she might as well start doing laundry. And you know what? That's exactly what she did one September afternoon after we were all in school.

She found herself done with therapies and home alone and decided to do some laundry.

Our laundry room is just off of our kitchen, separated by single-fold door with the fold coming into the kitchen. I would often times start a load of laundry and then pull the door closed so that the noise didn't interrupt the rest of the house (too much—it was just a single-fold door, after all).

On the afternoon of Mom's laundry adventure, she maneuvered herself (in her wheelchair) into the laundry room after several attempts. The door, when open, actually took up quite a bit of the doorway space and my mom's wheelchair, with the brakes on the side, actually took up quite a bit of the doorway space as well. But, she persevered, dragging the laundry basket behind her or pushing it ahead of her in order to get where she needed to be. She carefully and nervously stood up to retrieve the laundry soap above the washer and dropped a pod into the machine. Then she piled the dirty clothes into the washer and shut the lid.

Feeling quite happy with her return to a productive activity, even if it were laundry, she began pushing herself back in the direction from whence she came. The pantry is located directly across from the washer and dryer and the space between the panty and laundry is standard size. This is to say it's big enough for me to turn around in, but not big enough for a wheelchair to turn around, so she backed up.

And she backed herself right into the door and proceeded to close it on herself. She maneuvered her chair toward the garage door thinking she could maybe get turned around after all and she ended up tumping over the trash can before getting herself stuck. (Y'all know that tumping means turning over and dumping out the contents of said item, right? I spent about three hours one night schooling my Facebook friends on the usefulness of this word. Friend me on Facebook. I'm very educational.)

She picked up the trash and manipulated her wheelchair yet again attempting to get into a position that would allow her to pass through the doorway without ripping the folding door off of it's hinges. Eventually, she found herself stuck.

That's right, I said stuck. She couldn't leave the laundry room and all of her attempts at exiting left her truly stuck.

My mom eventually dug her phone from the purse that Courtney had gotten her and which my mom always carried around her neck. She called my sister.

The good news is that when my sister stopped laughing, she came into town and helped her. But not before getting herself stuck with Mom first.

The better news is that she finished her load of laundry.

That day, Mom was my hero. Not because she attempted to do something she wasn't sure she'd be able to accomplish—and she did it anyway. But more than that: she did my laundry for me.

I don't care who you are or what obstacles you have to cross: If you do my laundry I will call you a hero.

Any Typical Saturday Morning

I wake at eighty-ish. Brian is already up at 'em. He still believes that he lives on a farm where the cows must be fed, so he wakes up way earlier than I even knew existed. Chances are that he's in the living room, watching some history documentary on Netflix with his earbuds in.

I stretch and peer down the hall to discover that my mother is not in the bathroom. I assume she's still sleeping, so I play on Facebook and attempt to doze. My bladder hates me, though, and I have to get up to pee. Since I'm already up, I start a load of laundry. As I pass by the kitchen, I see that the dishwasher door is slightly ajar and smile because I assume that means someone has done the dishes for me. I silently cuss when I pull the door open a bit more and discover that no one has done jack squat as far as the dishes are concerned. I throw in a few stray dishes from the sink and start the dishwasher.

I peek in on my mom. She's still sleeping, but I notice that she's already dressed. She must have gotten up when Brian did.

I peek in on Brian, headphones are in and his brows are furrowed, indicating that he's deep in thought. Do I know my man or do I know my man?

Hadley is up shortly after me and comes dragging herself into the kitchen, where I'm putting a chicken on to boil to make chicken and noodles. "Can I watch *Criminal Minds* on the iPad?"

"What are you doing for breakfast?" I ask back.

"I'm not hungry," she mumbles as she grabs the iPad from the counter.

My mom wheels into the kitchen, "When'd you get up? I've been up since five."

I roll my eyes and tell her that I caught her back in bed, sleeping. "You may have gotten up at five, but you didn't stay up." She shrugs and puts her mug under the Keurig.

"What would you like for breakfast?" I ask her pouring myself a glass of orange juice.

"Oh, nothing big. Maybe just some eggs, bacon and toast," she says sincerely.

"How about a frog-in-the-hole*?" I ask trying to combine two tasks into one.

She nods approvingly, then moves to the table and begins reading her iPad.

"What about me?" Hadley mumbles still in her pajamas, clutching her iPad.

"You want a frog-in-the-hole?" I ask, still trying to make my job easier.

She rolls her eyes as only a teenager can and says two words, "Eww. Waffle."

I poke my head into the living room. "Want Breakfast?" I ask my lover. He ignores me.

I say it louder, "Want Breakfast?" His eyes don't even blink.

I walk right up to him and jiggle the computer in his lap. "Want breakfast?"

"Already had some," he says in a voice that is way too loud as he points to a plate, a bowl, a spoon and a fork.

I walk into the kitchen, his dishes in my hand, and hear our fairly quiet dishwasher change gears.

"The skillet's smoking," my mom announces. I turn the burner off and butter the bread for the frog-in-the-holes. I pour some waffle mix into a bowl and add some water. Really. I don't know the proper measurements—just *some*.

I unplug the Keurig and plug in the waffle iron.

I add the buttered bread to the skillet, cut the frog hole and break an egg into each piece of bread. I turn the burner back on.

I pour the waffle mix into the waffle iron, close it and flip it.

Briley stumbles into the kitchen. "Are you eating without me?"

"I'll make you breakfast. I'm making Nana and me a frog-in-the-hole and making Hadley a waffle."

"But you aren't making me anything?" Her chin quivers as she looks at the kitchen, filled with smoke.

"What do you want?" I sigh.

"A waffle."

I flip the frogs, pull the plates from the cabinet, grab the butter dish and open the waffle iron. I'm in the process of pouring another waffle when the dryer signal goes off.

"It's so funny to watch you jump," Briley says, grinning, knowing that her practical joke of the turned-on-dryer-signal works on me every single time.

Hadley wanders into the kitchen, "Momma, close one eye and stand on the opposite foot."

"I'm kinda cooking breakfast right now, Had," I sigh.

"I'll do it," Briley offers.

"No!" Hadley bellows at her sister. "I want Momma to do it."

"I can do it anyway. Let me do it."

My mom taps onto a video of Carrie Underwood belting out some old hymn and then asks over the blaring music, "Where's the volume on my iPad?"

Brian hollers from the living room, "Honey. You need to watch this show when you get done. I had no idea that the blahdy-blah family had a history of mental illness after the whatsy-whos took over their empire."

I set a frog-in-the-hole down in front of my mom, set waffles in front of my kids, and down the rest of my orange juice as I take my blood pressure medicine and happy pill.

I'm back in bed for a nap by 9:15.

*Frog In The Hole

I used to think this was a southern thing, but most of my southern friends crinkle their noses and say, "But, where's the bacon grease?"

Then a friend from Ohio posted that she loved "Toads" for breakfast and I was like, *Gross—only people from Louisiana eat frog legs.* And she was like, *No, these are eggs.*

Then a friend in California posted that her kids love "Hole Eggs" for breakfast and I was like *Hey! You're spelling it wrong.* And she was like, *Stop being so grammar-y all the time.*

And then there are some people who have no idea what any of us are talking about—this recipes for you.

1 egg

1 piece of bread

copious amounts of softened butter

Heat a griddle or skillet to medium while you butter both sides of the bread. Put the bread in the skillet and use a biscuit cutter to cut a whole in the bread. Put the cut hole in the skillet after you pull it from the center of the bread. Crack an egg into the hole in the bread. Salt and pepper to taste. Turn and toast/cook on the other side. When egg is done and toast is as desired, eat it.

Well, take it out of the skillet first. Or not. It's your breakfast.

My Wisconsin-born editor says this needs cheese.

And I say, "Sure. Why not."

So, add some cheese. Then eat it.

The Noises

If you've read any of my other stuff (and by stuff, I mean books, blogs, Facebook statuses, Tweets, writings on Tootsie's wall in Nashville), you'll know that our dogs, Bo and JJ are crazy. I often refer to Bo as The Dumb Dog, but let me be clear about this: He's a pretty sharp dog.

Our very first fur baby was Daisy. Daisy was so sweet and gentle and loving. We got her after a couple of years of trying in vain to have a human baby. She sat with me on the couch as I'd cry each month I wasn't pregnant. She was calm and tender around Hadley and Briley once they appeared on the scene. She was just a fabulous dog.

About the same time we wound up with Bo, Daisy began going blind. When we moved to our current home—with a pool—Daisy began going deaf. We did not train Daisy to walk around the pool and steer clear of it. We didn't necessarily teach Daisy where her dog house was or the food and water bowls. All of that was on Bo. He did all of that without being asked. Smart, huh? He still pestered the holy hell out of her, but he took care of her as well.

The veterinarian assured us that when it was time to put her down, we'd know because Daisy just wouldn't enjoy life any more. Her tail would fail to wag. She would stop responding to us. She might possibly be in pain from the glaucoma or from her eardrums bursting. We'd know, the vet said time and again, when it was time to tell her goodbye and let her go.

And one spring day, we knew. Bo took it harder than any of us. (Actually, Brian was quite upset, but that doesn't help my story flow, now does it?)

In response to losing Daisy and seeing poor Bo miserable, we rescued a black lab with hip dysplasia. We named him JJ.

I tell you all of this because when that time comes for my mom, we plan on driving her to the vet and having her put down humanely then getting a new Nana from Craigslist. It's our right under Obamacare. I read it on Facebook.

I'M KIDDING! I'M KIDDING!

I tell you all about Bo and JJ because as sweet and calming as Daisy was, JJ is not. Add to that Bo's alpha dog, gotta-be-in-charge attitude and they are quite the pair. One Saturday morning, while I was home alone and still in my pajamas, they locked me out of the house. *They* being the dogs, donchaknow. And I think they did it on purpose

And while Bo is large and in charge of the canine branch of the family tree, he's a scared-y cat when it comes to rain and storms and threats of rain or storms. Even though we live in Oklahoma—where we've been under drought conditions since, well, before the Dust Bowl—we do get quite a few rainstorms.   The good news is this: If we aren't home, Bo can open the door. We have a pull-down handle and he just opens the back door and lets himself in.

Unless the door is locked.

In that case, he'll climb our fence to the neighbor's yard, army crawl under a low spot in their fence and come around to our front door and let himself in.

Unless that door is locked.

At which time he'll go through the hole he scratched through our garage door and let himself in through the garage.

The dog hates storms.

When Daisy was alive, she'd get in her doghouse and ride it out if we weren't home to let her in. Bo learned nothing from our sweet Daisy.

With JJ, he blindly follows Bo (not literally, like poor, sweet Daisy did), and JJ then digs in the trash, wags his fifty-pound tail, licks your butt and loves you as you yell about the trash all over the house.

I know you think I've accidently slipped a chapter in here from my forthcoming book, "Crap You Never Wanted To Know About My Dogs." But, all of this is important to the point of this particular story and it has to do with sex.

(See? Makes sense, right?)

Maybe I need to explain more.

So, one night we went to bed without checking the weather. Bo tried to let himself in the back door. I can only imagine that JJ was standing behind him wagging his tail salivating about our trashcan.

The door however was locked, so ...

Bo headed to the front door. About six months before, we got a new garage door, which was made of metal, and Bo hadn't quite figured out how to make his own doggy door. So, he stood on our front stoop beating the heck out of door trying to get it to open.

It was about four in the morning when I half-woke up thinking that someone was breaking into our house. Hearing the rain through my open window and quickly deduced that the noise was not a very loud and clumsy boogieman. Obviously, Bo was at one of the doors. I nudged Brian. Brian should let him in, I reasoned as I snuggled into my pillow yet again, on the off chance that it was a loud and clumsy boogieman.

Brian rolled over and threw his arm around me. I threw it right back. "Go get the door," I grumbled.

Brian rolled back over and threw his legs over the bed and mumbled, "That dog drives me insane."

To be fair, it's not just the dog that makes him insane ...

But, he let Bo in (and JJ) and they went merrily to the dog room (which is sometimes called a craft room or a sewing room or an ante room by normal people with sane dogs).

Brian crawled back in bed with me, threw his arm over me once again and began snoring.

The next morning, the sun was out because it is Oklahoma, and Oklahoma is where Mother Nature comes to skitz out on crack. I sat at the breakfast table with my mom (Remember her? The subject of this whole book?), and we looked out into the back yard where I had just let the dogs out to gallivant through the puddles.

"Dumb dogs," I muttered.

"Why?" she asked turning more toward the window to see some unknown dumb thing.

"Stupid Bo just about beat down the door last night once the rain started," I explained.

"He did?" she questioned. "I don't think I heard him."

"Really?" I asked, wistful that my mom could've slept deep like that when I missed curfew.

"Really."

"WOW. I thought he was going to knock the entire front part of the house down."

"Oh! I think I did hear that," she nodded serenely as if the Dali Lama himself had just passed on the secret to a happy life. I sipped my orange juice then tried not to spit it all over her when she said, "But, I thought it was yours and Brian's sex noises."

Let's Talk About Sex Noises
The one where I left no euphemistic phrase unturned

It's safe to say that regardless of how old or how married one is, it's difficult to really get into the act of making love with ones partner while one's mother is under the same roof. Brian has always asserted that getting jiggy wit' it in one of our old high school bedrooms is really hot. I assert that the chance for any parent, real, in-law, fictional or otherwise, to walk in while I'm in a compromising (albeit enjoyable) position(s) is not really that hot to me. Not really hot at all. #truth

Actually, the idea that I am caught with my pants down, literally, does nothing for me.

That's why establishing oneself in one's own dwelling is such an important part of maturing. Well, that and being independent, learning to budget, meal planning, and balance one's time are important as well. But, I think it's safe to say that mostly, young adults branch out on their own to get some unmonitored nookie. I mean independence. Yeah, independence. It has nothing to do with getting naked with other people.

Brian and I have always had a very healthy and enjoyable intimate life. Even after almost twenty-years of marriage, we make things work and keep the spark alive. (Don't believe me? Read my award-winning book, *Getting Lucky*, available on Amazon.com.)

The months between my mom's stroke and her moving in with us were lean times in the bedroom. I was working, spending time with my mom, cleaning out her house, taking care of my mom's business with my sister. Brian was working, taking care of the house, running the girls to the golf course, the softball fields, to tournaments and back home again. We were barely kissing each other goodnight.

I knew that having my mom at our house would be better on our schedules. She could be a part of our lives, and we'd get to visit with her whenever we wanted. I was feeling the relief wash over me the week or so before she came home.

The night before her arrival into the house we call home, her room was ready. Since the master toilet in our bedroom was the best one suited for her needs, she would be using that one. With the shower bars and raised toilet seat installed, that was ready. Most of her items were put away. We were all ready to have her home. This would be a great change for us in our lives.

As Brian and I fell into bed that night, he leaned over to me, pulling me to him and said, "This may be the last night we get to do this for a while."

"Do what?" I asked him, my interest piqued. (I may have been all kinds of tired by this point in the journey.)

"Bump uglies." Brian had always had a thing for euphemisms.

"Wait," I put my hand on his chest in a effort to pause his actions, but not stop them completely. "Why won't we be able to do this for a while?"

"Your mom will be here, and she'll be using our bathroom, and you are kinda loud."

Let me just stop right here and explain that while I may be "kinda loud," I have it on good authority (not a video, if that's what you're thinking) that I am not beat-down-the-door loud. I wouldn't even know how to make the sounds that mimic someone or something beating down a door. It'd be kinda cool if I did know how to make that sound, though, kinda like the guy on Police Academy.

Also, if I did make sounds like that I'm sure that Brian would go around the country—maybe even the world!—and give seminars entitled "How To Make Your Woman Sound Like She's Beating Down A Door During Sex: A Practical Set Of Instructions For Husbands, Boyfriends, Partners And Lesbian Lovers." And he would be proud to do it.

But, back to the story of not doing the horizontal hop for a while ...

"Well," I offered, "We'll just have to figure out the best time." Then, we did some mattress dancing wherein I kept my volume in check.

So, let me set the stage, so to speak, for you. I believe this will also answer some questions for you as well.

We do have a door on our bedroom. We use it.

We also have a lock on the door as well. We used it until, one night as we rested in post-coital bliss, fully covered (thank goodness) our door slammed open as Briley walked right up to our bed and announced that Snoopy was in the room. Then she peed and went back to her room. She's a sleepwalker. It was that night that we realized our lock was busted. Not because of Briley. It probably never worked. It looks good, though.

We could replace the lock, but with my mom coming to visit us and needing to have access to the bathroom, it wouldn't be smart.

We also have ceramic tile in the hall and the bathroom, so we can hear the pitter-patter of little feet and the squinch-squinch of rubber wheels approaching our room. So, really, we have a little bit of notice when we're about to be interrupted. But, c'mon. Who among us likes to spend half of his/her flesh session with his/her ear to the ground, metaphorically speaking. Unless, of course, that's the particular position you were going for.

We tried to find other locations to lift a leg and lay some pipe. As a matter of fact, my mom's house was empty. But, my sister had been busy packing it up, so it pretty much looked like an warehouse after a tornado had blown through it following a good ransacking by a team of toddler thugs. Plus, when the neighbors see my car in my mom's driveway, they all come over asking about my mom and offering their help. One time, I started to pay a little neighbor kid five bucks if he would just give us five uninterrupted minutes.

We were going to need to do the horizontal hula at home. So, we turned into the *Criminal Minds* BAU team. We noticed that Hadley went to sleep quickly and soundly (with the help of Melatonin, of course). Briley was a sleepwalker about midnight for a couple of hours. Mom would use the restroom about three and at almost five. Our alarm went off at six. Hadley woke up at seven without fail or alarm.

With that profile in place, we figured that anytime after two until three or from 5:45 to six.

Some nights (or mornings), depending on our schedule, the two to three a.m. slot worked well. Most ~~nights~~ mornings, the 5:45 time was our time to take a turn in the stubble.

This actually turned out to be an ideal time for us. When the deed had been done, Brian would take a shower and get his morning started. I would hit snooze until the last possible moment and then rush around frantically trying to get ready on time.

Then one morning, we were savoring a shake in the sheets when literally, our sheets began shaking.

"OHMYGOODNESS!" I called out, concerned that a kid or a mom had made their way to our bed without our knowledge, but feeling kinda excited that I was that in the zone to not notice.

I hopped out of bed to find no one. Weird.

"What?" Brian gasped breathlessly.

"I thought someone was on the bed."

"We are," he grinned and patted the space beside him. Quickly checking the clock and realizing that we still had time, I snuggled beside him again and quickly found our groove again. Then lost it just as quickly by the same bed bumping that wasn't coming from me or Brian.

"Did you feel that?" I whispered and lay perfectly still.

"I felt the earth move, baby," Brian said, quoting sensual 70s song lyrics. Then he screamed.

Now, as vocal as I supposedly am while visiting the happy valley, Brian is not. So, to have him scream like that meant that he was either in pain, or he was having an aneurism.

Then his vocals continued, "Damn cats!" And I saw our tuxedo cat claw his way up to the top of Brian's gyrating head.

The BAU never has to contend with sneaky, early-rising cats.

P.S. My mom slept through Brian's yells. So did the girls. When Brian got out of the shower, both cats were asleep on his pillow.

P.P.S. Brian says make an offer on the cats.

P.P.P.S. That's not true; he'll give them to you along with a half-full box of liter.

Girls Gone Wild
or Girls Gone Wild in the West
or Girls Gone Wild in the Super Duper Hellmart Club

Labor Day weekend found us in a weird situation. One of our southern niece's birthday party was that weekend in southern Oklahoma. (Our southern nieces live at the southern border of Oklahoma. Our northern niece lives at the northern border.) My sister and brother-in-law's anniversary was also that weekend, and they planned to go to Branson as they always do. In year's past, my family would travel south. My sister's family would travel east. And our mom would stay in town and probably go buy three-hundred dollars worth of crap she already had from Hellmart.

This year, with the birthday and anniversary dates not changing, we found ourselves in a bit of a quandary since my mom couldn't be left home alone just yet due to her stroke. And perhaps quandary is too big of a word. It was just a situation we'd have to navigate. Because I was not important to the birthday party nor was I important to the anniversary plans, I gave my blessing for everyone to leave town, and I stayed back with Mom.

The first night, Friday night, I went and got burgers at my favorite burger joint, Lot-A-Burger. I'm not sure where I went wrong, but no one else in my family appreciates the greasy goodness in the same manner that I do. So, I went all out and ordered myself a double-meat, double cheese burger, no tomatoes add extra onions.

Oh my ground beef goodness. When the onions are sliced oh-so thin, put on the bun and topped with thin, steamy, greasy patties and then lettuce and pickles are piled high before the top bun is added ... Mercy! Sure it's a heart attack waiting to happen, but what a way to go. My gosh! If ever I'm on death row, my last meal will be about a dozen of these greasy mounds of manna and hope that the good Lord takes me just before I take the final bite. Gracious how I love these burgers! If ever you're in town, let's go grab one together, okay?

And maybe while we're eating our square meal on a round bun, as they are often referred to, I'll remember where I was going with this story.

Oh yeah.

Labor Day.

I got my mom and me Lot-A-Burger and brought it back home. We ate our meal at the table then watched a couple of shows on the television set before we turned in for the night. As we ate, my mom asked a few questions that at the time seemed really benign, very small talkish. Things like *Is the new CVS open?* or *What's it like outside? Anything new? Is the grass even still green?*

As I lay in bed that night scrolling through Facebook and watching *Orange Is The New Black* on Netflix (this may or may not have been the real reason I volunteered to stay home by myself on this particular weekend), it hit me that my mom had not really been out of the house, aside from doctors' appointments, since we sprung her from The Village. Right then and there, I decided that the next day we'd get out and go to town. But first, I needed to finish Pennsatuky's story line in Season 2.

Now, when I say *go to town*, I do not mean that we hung out in our little town and hit up Hellmart to grab a few pizza rolls for dinner. Why? Because I already knew that we were going to have Lot-A-Burger for dinner again.

What I meant when I said we were going to go to town was that we were going to head down south and go to the Super-Duper Hellmart Club and buy fifty-pounds of pizza rolls. Don't worry—I was still planning on eating at Lot-A-Burger.

The first thing I had to do, though, was text my sister and ruin her weekend, of course.

Me: FYI: I'm taking Mom shopping at Super Duper Hellmart Club.

Rachel: Are you sure? I'm not sure she's up to it.

Me: I'm sure. In fact, I'm so sure, we're going to the Super Duper Hellmart Club in Branson with you.

Rachel: No you're not.

Me: Sure I am—Mom's got a credit card.

I didn't hear anymore from my sister. Sometimes she ignores me for no good reason at all.

Saturday morning, we slowly got around. My mom was slow because she's had a stroke. I was slow because it was Saturday, and I didn't have to be fast. I told my mom of my plans for us to go shopping, and she picked up her pace. I, however, did not. Breakfast became brunch and shortly thereafter, we loaded up and headed south.

Now, since my mom had not even been to a regular-sized Hellmart since her stroke, I was a little bit nervous about how, exactly, we would forge our way through the super store. The thought of an electric cart crossed my mind, but it had not been so long since my mom drove that I quickly dismissed it. Plus, electronics are just inside the front doors of our Super-Duper Hellmart Club. Sure, my mom had a credit card, but I was certain the credit limit couldn't cover a runaway electric cart crashing into a grouping of wide-screens. I also have quite an affinity for free samples on Saturday afternoon, and I didn't want to risk being banned for life.

So, with all of these considerations, I decided that we'd just leave mom in her own chair. Easy enough.

Unless we wanted to buy stuff.

And we did want to buy stuff. We wanted to buy lots of stuff. In case I haven't mentioned it, my mom had a credit card.

Now, I'm not an engineer. I've not even taken any engineering classes, but I am a problem solver, so I devised a plan: I put a cart in front of my mom, who was sitting in her wheelchair. She'd use her left hand to steer the cart, and I'd push her in the chair.

Truly, this was a great plan. Except that sometimes I'd say let's go left, and my mom would go left but I really meant to say let's go right, and she wasn't reading my mind and then a whole pyramid of industrial-sized barrels of cheese balls would roll down aisles 12, 13, 14 and 15. The first fifteen minutes we were in the Super-Duper Hellmart Club were spent sounding like this, *Turn left, no, I mean right. Um. Excuse us. Sorry. Here, let me get this. Oh shoot, I'll pick this up. Sorry, excuse me. Turn right, no, I mean left...*

My mom objected when I put my purse strap in her mouth like a horse's bit and directed her steering that way. Clearly, having a stroke had made her less of a team player. With a lot of slow movements and a lot of holding my hands out in front of my face to see which thumb and index finger formed an L, we were able to get our ninety-two rolls of toilet paper, fifty-six pounds of pizza rolls and enough Gatorade to last through the NFL playoffs—for both teams. And it only took us two hours and seventeen minutes.

I loaded up the back of the minivan and loaded up my mom and crawled into the driver's seat utterly exhausted.

"You know, Heather?" My mom said, "That was a lot of fun—even though I didn't appreciate your fish-hooking my mouth with your finger and yelling, *giddy-up* when we were turning down the spices aisle."

"But Mom! There were only three cases of chipotle lemon pepper salt left!" I protested. Some people don't understand the urgency of bulk shopping.

"I'm so glad you brought me out, Heather," she continued, "It's been a long time since I felt normal and today, I felt normal again."

This made me tear up a little bit. And not just because I was afraid that being treated like a plow horse was *normal* for my mom.

But enough about horses.

I looked over at my mom and said, "I'm glad you had a good time."

"Oh, I did, Heather! I did! Now, let's go get something to eat. But first, I have to use the bathroom."

The First Time in A Public Bathroom
Yes, A Public Bathroom
More Specifically, A Public Bathroom With MY Mom

My mom had her knee replaced about twenty or so years ago. She went through intense physical therapy and finally, after years and years and years of not being able to walk with any kinda of stability, she could at least walk sorta stabily. Stabily? Stably? *(*Editor's Note: Stably. Unless she walked with knives or a particular attitude, then stabbily would work.)*

Whatever—she could walk better after her replacement and therapy.

My aunt Kay, however, thought she needed more support. I honestly can think of very few things that make me shake my head at my aunt Kay. In fact, I can only think of two times she's made me furrow my brow: One was when we were all in a hotel room in St. Louis and she wouldn't let me change the channel from *M*A*S*H* even though no one at all was watching it. The other was when she bought my mom a toilet seat riser after my mom's knee replacement surgery.

That's right, my friends, my aunt gave my mom a toilet seat riser.

Now, I'm not sure exactly why this miffed me so much, but it did. It not only miffed me, but it miffed my sister as well. I mean, our house was never a showcase home, but this toilet seat riser certainly did nothing to help the situation.

Fast forward to June 2014.

My sister and I set out on a shopping trip in our smallish metropolis. Our first stop was the local home-health supply store.

I had my bathroom measurements on a note in my phone ... and we were looking for (that's right) toilet seat risers.

"What happened to that one that Aunt Kay got her?" I asked my sister.

She shrugged, "That was over twenty years ago."

"I know that," I scoffed, like toilet seat risers ever go out of style. "But what happened to it, though?"

Again she shrugged.

You know? It's not like one can shove a toilet seat riser to the back of a closet or donate it to a second-hand store. Or can you? Maybe we should have checked out the second-hand store before going to the home health store. But, that would have been gross, right? (The answer is right. It would have been yucky, totally and unbelievably gross.)

So, putting my cheap notions aside, on that sunny June day, we set out to purchase a toilet seat riser for my mom. This would be the second one she had owned in her lifetime. Surely that's a record. But, when Mom came home, she had to have a place to, ya know, *go*. And more importantly, she had to have a way to get up when she was done going. We spared no expense—and I'm not just saying that because the second-hand store didn't even have one in stock—we got the toilet seat riser that had arms on the side and could double as a shower seat. Living the life, y'all.

We go all kinds of fancy with our geriatric home décor, y'all.

While learning to use the bathroom at home came with a wide curve, it was easily conquered. In no time at all, Mom could use the facilities without any help from me and eventually without any supervision.

(I know that all you moms out there wonder when you'll be able to go to the bathroom without an audience of off-spring. Well, I know when that will happen: From the time your children get married right up until you have a stroke.)

And, on that fateful Labor Day weekend when my mom and I set out to take the Super Duper Hellmart Club by storm, I didn't give one single thought to emptying our bladders. This is ironic because my bladder is rivaled in size only by a single English sweet pea.

So, I was taken aback when my mom announced she had to see a man about a horse.

She didn't really say that—in fact, she hates that euphemism. In fact, she'll probably read this section and say, "Lands, Heather. I didn't even think that much less say it."

I thought briefly about driving home at an alarming rate of speed so that she could use the fancy-schmancy toilet seat riser. But, she had already promised me that she'd pay at the Cracker Barrel if we got there before the dinner prices started.

Since I was apparently concerned with eating at Cracker Barrel, I decided to take our chances with the handicapped bathroom there.

I completely understand that practically every public place has to have a handicapped restroom facility. But, I also understand that not every handicapped restroom facility is easily used. In fact, my mom, whose right side was left impaired following her stroke, cannot easily use a facility that has the handicap bars on the right side of the toilet.

Also, not every toilet sits high, And since her knees were weak to begin with and now her right leg lacks the strength to be able to easily stand up from a low-situation seat, a lot of public toilets leave her too low in order to successfully stand up from the can. (If y'all listen closely, you can hear my mother say, "Oh, gads! I didn't say can!" And it's true: She is fond of the word *commode*.)

But, we had to take our chances: I pulled into the parking lot at the Cracker Barrel and helped my mom from the van to her wheelchair. I maneuvered her through Ye Ol' Country Store (which is not hip friendly much less wheelchair friendly) without knocking over (too) many items. We propped open the bathroom door while we wheeled into the bathroom.

Good news! The handicapped bars were on the left side. I breathed easier as I got my mom into the stall and positioned her so that she could use the loo. (She's not British—she'd never really say loo.)

All of this build up to get us actually into the toilet stall and you know what? Nothing major happens, aside from, ya know, peeing and stuff. But, wait—there's more! I get to annoy my sister.

I whipped out my phone from my back pocket and texted my sister; it had been, after all, a few hours since I'd tormented her.

Me: Guess what!
Rachel: Oh no. What now?
Me: Mom's going to the bathroom.
Rachel: Good, I guess??
Me: In Cracker Barrel. She's using a public bathroom.

Rachel: Why are you in Cracker Barrel?

Me: To go to the bathroom.

Rachel: No, I mean, are you going to eat there too?

Me: Nope ... just going to the bathroom. Give me a minute and I'll send you a pic.

Rachel: I'm deleting your number.

She didn't delete my number.

I didn't send her a picture.

I Instagrammed it instead.

Not everyone has a picture of her mom on the ceramic throne.

Yes, Mom. Commode. I know.

Potty Training:
My Toddlers vs. My Mom

I remember the day*S* (that's plural, y'all), I potty trained my older daughter, Hadley. She turned two in November and put on the big girl panties. She did great! She was very leery of going poop in the potty, but eventually, she learned that it wasn't nearly as bad as she thought it was. Then, I had Briley in January and was home with a newborn who was getting her diaper changed all the time. So ... we started the potty training process with Hadley again. In March, I went back to work, and back to potty training with Hadley. So many transitions! Looking back, I wouldn't have potty trained Hadley until I was off for summer break in May—which is when her potty training actually stuck.

Briley, since she was a different kid, had a different potty training experience. Learning from her big sister, I waited until the summer after she turned two. For a couple of weeks in June, she would change her own diapers. So, we switched her to Pull-Ups, which she also changed. So, we switched her to big girl panties—which she would replace with Pull-Ups when she had to go potty. In July, I got very sick with Rocky Mountain Spotted Fever. If you don't have ticks in your neck of the woods, could I come live with you? If you do have ticks in your neck of the woods, you'll know of this ugly Rocky Mountain Spotted Fever.

On about day three of being icky, Brian took Hadley out during nap time. Briley was supposedly down for a nap, and I was lying on the couch, watching TV wondering why Oprah hadn't paid someone to rid the world of ticks yet. I heard the tiny patter of toddler feet coming to the living room.

"Momma?" a tiny Briley called out pulling a package of Pull-Ups with her. "You will help me pull dem up?"

"No," I said as I wept with exhaustion, "Momma's not doing this anymore. You have to wear big girl panties and you have to use the toilet."

"Oh," she said as she nodded her head. She went right to the bathroom, sat herself upon the Elmo toilet set and went potty like a big girl. We didn't have any issues after that.

The next day, after a full-day of no accidents (and having to remind her only once), we celebrated the end of our diaper days with an antibiotic shot and a double dose of Motrin. I was still sick, ya know.

And that ended my potty training days.

Fast forward almost ten years and ... my mom had her stroke.

Like I mentioned earlier, stroke patients all have some sort of bladder issue as a result of their incident. In most cases, it's just a little hiccup. In some cases, like my Mom's case, it is life-changing.

When Mom was at The Village, part of her therapy was to relearn when she had to go to the bathroom and to independently use the toilet. In the meantime, my mom traded in her Victoria's Secret Undergarments* for adult diapers. This potty learning appeared to be going somewhat smoothly ... while the therapists were there. But, as she slept, it was easier for the night staff to just change my mom's pants while my mom was still in bed. Eventually, my mom learned to sleep through these middle-of-the-night potty breaks. If there were an accident that the staff didn't catch, they'd just change the bed when she got up the next morning to go to therapy.

When she was liberated from The Village, they did not send any staff home with her, which was almost a deal breaker for me.

Since Mom came home in July, both Brian and I were home; school didn't start until mid-August. At the end of the first week, I was a little bit weary from doing a load of bedding every single morning, but it took me almost three full weeks before I decided there had to be an easier way.

"So, did you have these bladder issues at The Village?" I sighed, shutting the small laundry room door.

"Yes. I think I did." This is when she confessed to me how they would change her each night. This is also when I silently cursed my lack of staff.

"How do you feel about rubber sheets?" I asked my mom one morning over breakfast, the spin cycle serenading us as it had every single morning since Mom came home.

"I don't think there is such a thing, is there?" I heard her say as I dozed off to sleep over my eggs. I was used to sleeping until noon in July, after all.

The "easier" way came to me in the middle of the night: If this was when my mom's bladder gave out, then this is when we needed to wake her up to potty.

I remember knowing that Hadley needed to go at noon every day without fail. At 11:50, we'd usher her to the bathroom and stay dry. That same philosophy would work with my seventy-five year old mom as well.

That night as I fell into bed at around midnight, I set my alarm for three a.m., which was really, really hard to do. I love sleep, but I'm not very good at it. And when I wake up, it's not easy for me to go back to sleep. So, my concern here was that I would be getting about three hours of sleep. Total. (Yes, I know I could go to bed earlier, but then you wouldn't be reading this book because without my burning the midnight oil, I would rarely get a word written.)

That first night, my alarm went off, and I jumped out of bed as if the house were on fire. I spun around aimlessly a couple of times trying to remember why my alarm would be going off at three in the friggin' morning. My bladder decided that would be a good time to empty itself, so I went to the bathroom and that's when I remembered: *Wake Mom up.*

It took a few moments to get my mom up. Then it took a few more to get my mom to stop cussing. A few more minutes to get her out of bed, into her chair and heading toward the bathroom. Eventually she got the job done and was back in bed. I checked my phone: 3:52.

The next night, I only spun around twice and my mom only cussed under her breath and we shaved seven minutes off of our time.

The next night, I hit snooze, skipped the confused spinning, ignored the cussing, and we were done within thirty minutes.

Eventually, right around the time school started back (which proves that the universe is on my side), my mom could wake up on her own, get herself to the bathroom and get herself back in bed.

Nonetheless, it's easier to potty train your toddler, than to potty train your momma.

*My mom has never owned Victoria's Secret Undergarments. But, admitting that she wore spandex, tummy control granny panties didn't sound quite as ~~sexy~~ funny.

Why Potty Training Your Mom is Like Potty Training Your Toddler

- Stickers on a chart are a waste of good stickers and charts.
- Once you get your subject on the pot, you cannot wander far until the deed is done.
- Suggesting a trip to the toilet is bound to be a interruption (respectively of either playtime or *The Meredith Vieira Show*).
- You must pack extra clothing—not only for the trainee but the trainer as well.
- You will go through copious amounts of toilet paper and not understand why or how.
- Neither toddler nor stroke patient will appreciate your singing voice when you belt out "The Pee Pee Song."
- Both toddlers and moms will try to hide all evidence of an accident.
- Bribing with M & Ms is still a sure fire way to get a tinkle.

Going High-Tech

It wasn't too long before my mom needed to go to the Super Duper Hellmart Club again. And, truthfully, couldn't one go there every single day and find something to buy in bulk? (Yes, the answer is yes.)

"But, this time, Heather, I want to try the electronic cart."

If this had been a scene in a television show, the music would've changed to a minor key and the camera would've zoomed in on my face wincing in horror. Then we would've cut to a commercial, leaving the home audiences to ponder how this partially paralyzed stroke patient would be able to maneuver an electric cart.

When the show resumed, the scene would've been me and my momma in the entry way to the

Super Duper Hellmart Club, sizing up the electronic carts. My mom's face would've been filled with thoughts of freedom and excitement. Mine would've showed the same wincing-in-horror face from before the commercial. If the camera panned out, it would have revealed me standing with my legs crossed, one in front of the other, trying to keep myself from peeing my pants and oddly enough craving M & Ms with all the anxiety of my mother getting behind the wheel—sorta—for the first time since her stroke.

"Okay, Mom, just be careful and read the rules. Also, don't go too fast and be careful getting on the thing and don't get wild. Read all the instructions before we go and don't hit anything or anyone."

While I was still cautioning my mom and clenching my kegels, she had maneuvered herself from her wheelchair onto the electronic chair and was moving toward the front doors.

I grabbed my cart and followed lest she get too far ahead of me. After a few moments when I realized that she knew what she was doing, I whipped out my phone and snapped a picture. As she drove toward the pharmaceutical area (which is where the bathroom is located), I texted the picture to my sister, my aunt Kay and my uncle John.

My sister texted back: Don't let her do any damage.

Aunt Kay texted back: NASCAR, here she comes!

My uncle John called. But since I was en route to the restroom, and by enroute, I mean I was running and chanting *Don't Pee! Don't Pee! Don't Pee!*, I let it go to voice mail.

When my bladder was feeling relieved, I returned to the pharmaceutical area, dialed my uncle John's number and handed it to my mom.

My mom had maneuvered the cart to the side and I sat down on the bench and waited for her conversation to be finished so we could get on with our trip and buy all the jumbo sized boxes of flavored coffee creamer.

As my mother and Uncle John chatted back and forth, another lady in another electronic cart headed our way. She wanted to get by, obviously, and my mom, with only one workable hand, couldn't really keep a hold of the phone and move the cart. I whispered to my mom, "Don't worry" right before I stood up in front of my mother's cart and said, "Excuse us," to the impatient lady wanting to pass.

I reached out to my mom's hand controls and twisted them in an attempt to move her cart over to the side so people could pass easily. And that's when it hit me.

The cart, that is.

The cart hit me.

In essence, I ran over myself.

I ended up on my tail right in front of my mom's cart.

"Holy cow, Mom!" I cried as I tried to gracefully get up from the floor.

My mom laughed and said, "Heather just ran over herself!"

The lady in the other cart announced, with clear disdain for the whole situation in her voice, "I still can't get by."

I gathered a few things that had fallen from my purse and placed them along with my purse on the bench as I hoisted myself back to my feet. "Sorry," I mumbled as I reached out to my mom's hand controls, twisted the knob and ran myself over yet again!

Again, I found myself on my butt on the floor.

Again, my mother laughed herself silly.

Again, the lady in the other electric cart huffed, completely fed up with my one-woman slapstick show. But, she was able to pass and that's what's important here, right?

It's also important to note that I gave my mom and my uncle John a hearty laugh. I also supplied my aunt Kay and cousins, Courtney and Whitney, with much reason to giggle. And the pharmacist didn't even try to hide her laughter at my antics.

Plus, I'm pretty sure that the security guys monitoring the store security cameras were uploading my little slice of film to YouTube before I even found myself on my feet again.

Eventually, I texted my sister: Mom didn't do any damage.

It was the truth. Clearly my mom had (and still has) no problem with fancy-schmancy electric shopping carts. I, on the other hand, have quite a ways to go before I could be trusted with one.

That's Not How We Do It

Aunt Kay came to visit regularly. She still does as far as that goes. We all looked forward to her making the trip up north. Still do as far as that goes.

At the very least, she provided good visits for my mom while we were at school. But, she also liked to help my sister and me as much as she could. And as a bonus, she'd usually bring food. This is always good. Unless it's that healthy cookie recipe—woof! You know the cookies (if they can even be called that) I'm taking about, right? It made the rounds on Facebook. Yeah, those that you've pinned to your board "Healthy Cookies To Help Me Look Great In A Bikini." Yeah—those cookies. My aunt made them and brought them up one trip. Those "cookies" look like no-bake cookies, but they are full of smashed bananas, cinnamon and dirty sock juice. I don't want to say that I didn't like them, but I did spit my first bite out *at* my aunt Kay.

So, while she did (sometimes) bring good food, we also didn't bank on it. Often times, we'd go out. On one of my aunt Kay's visits, we decided to go to Dink's Pit Bar-B-Que for dinner. Dink's is a local, hometown favorite, smoking their own meat in a pit at the back of the dining area. Interesting fact about Dink's: I worked there as a hostess and a waitress. I was a brilliant hostess. I sucked as a waitress. I would also answer the phone by saying, "Dink *Spit* Bar-B-Que" because I could, and I thought it was funny.

That's not the point of this story, though.

The point is that my aunt Kay would come up and help us out as she could. And one night, as we headed to Dink's to eat us some Bar-B-Que, she decided to be helpful.

I parked the van in the handicapped spot as Briley was chatting endlessly (as she often does), and Hadley had her face in her phone (as she often does). Aunt Kay was chatting with Mom and I hopped out and headed to the back of the minivan to get the wheel chair out. Kay quickly joined me at the back, taking the chair from me and said, "I'll get her."

As she disappeared to the front of the van, Hadley leaned over the back seat and began telling me all about her new pretend boyfriend, Ed Sheeran, and the songs he sang for her. Briley was still chatting it up with Aunt Kay, and Aunt Kay was attending to my mom. Since it's a rare day that finds Hadley with her face away from the phone and willing to talk to me, I took full advantage to hear all about this ginger with the "like, way, way cool music." Hadley finished her rave on the top ten Ed Sheeran songs, and I closed the hatch to the minivan.

Walking to the passenger side of the van, I found Briley sitting half in and half out of the van, telling Aunt Kay about the latest pitch she was learning for softball and Aunt Kay being an attentive listener. I smiled because I've always liked my aunt Kay, and I knew that she'd always be an important part of our lives, no matter what happened with my mom.

And speaking of my mom ...

Where was she?

This was a mid-fall evening, so the sun had already set, but it was not quite what I'd consider dark yet. The parking lot lights had just turned on, though, so we could see. And what I could see was that my mom's wheelchair wasn't at the van.

Hadley, however, verbalized it best when she said, "What's Nana doing?"

The three of us, Aunt Kay, Briley and I, all looked back at Hadley who was staring off into the distance.

"What do you mean?" I asked.

She answered my question with a question of her own, "Where's Nana going?"

The three of us, Aunt Kay, Briley and I, all looked away from Hadley and into the distance, following Hadley's gaze.

What we found was my mom, in her wheelchair, rolling away across the parking lot away from Dink's Pit Bar-B-Que.

"OH!" My aunt hollered as she took off sprinting toward my mom.

"Wait!" I hollered trotting to my mom in her speed demon of a wheel chair.

"What's she doing?" hollered Hadley as she continued to stand beside the minivan because Hadley doesn't move fast for anyone.

"I'll just tell you about the drop ball once we get inside!" hollered Briley, not missing a beat in her conversation.

My aunt Kay and I arrived at my mom's side at about the same time. I'm not going to name names, but one of us was completely out of breath and one of us could speak without wheezing. Okay, fine. I'm so out of shape that a twenty-yard jog caused my ears to ring and my lungs to collapse in on themselves.

"What are you doing?" Aunt Kay asked.

I added my own two cents worth, "Yeah [huff,huff] what? [huff, huff]"

"I thought you were pushing me and I couldn't figure out what was going on," my mom replied looking right at her little sister. "I did notice that something must not be right when I didn't see your shadow behind my chair and when you wouldn't answer my questions."

It was then that we—all three of us—began to laugh.

It was also then that I decided when my aunt Kay says she'll help, I should also provide instructions.

How To Get My Mom Out Of The Car

1. Lock the wheels on the wheelchair.
2. Stand by the door.
3. Double check wheel locks.
4. Pay attention.
5. Don't unlock the wheels until you are ready to move away from the car.
6. Do not let go of the unlocked wheelchair no matter how enticing the conversation of an eleven-year-old is.

Other Things That Are Weird When You're In A Wheelchair

Handicapped Parking Spaces—You can't just park
in any handicapped space; you have to find the
one that will allow you the most room to
maneuver around the van. And sometimes you
have to re-park like you've been driving drunk
in order to keep the space reserved for you.

Handicapped Bathrooms—Since my mom can't use
her right hand, any handicapped bathroom that
has the bar on the right side is worthless for her.
But, I'll always use it because once I get in the
vicinity of a toilet, my bladder thinks it's go time.

Electric Carts—You have to be careful when you
park your regular wheel chair when using an
electric cart to shop. Someone will use your
personal chair even though it has your name
plastered all over it. And you will have to wait
until he finishes shopping before you can
actually leave the store. (True Story—I'm glad
my sister was with my mom when it happened
or I'd have just left her. Kidding. Sorta.)

Restaurants—not every place has tables and chairs
 and not every table is in a convenient place for
 you to park your wheelchair.
Pushing your mom in a wheel chair is not weird.
 Pulling on her ear to indicate which way you are
 turning is. And, apparently, it can be
 misconstrued as elder abuse. Whatevs.

Wheelchairs—They're Not Just For The Stroke Patient Anymore

Mom eventually got to a point where she was pretty much self-sufficient in our home, save for the rotten right sock that was just impossible to put on without both hands.

So, it was nothing at all for me to come in from school and ~~collapse on the couch~~ cook a healthy, nutritious dinner for my family while the girls ~~fought like Israelis and Palestinians~~ did their homework and Brian waited for new levels to open up on that infuriating Two Dots game. (There's really nothing more important that he could've been doing.) Typically, my mom would sit at the kitchen table and pretend to listen to the events of my day while really reading whatever book she was into.

There was one particularly weird fall afternoon wherein we all came home, as usual. I plopped on the couch, the girls commenced their fighting, and Brian bemoaned the fact that Two Dots hadn't added any new levels in well over three days. (Gah!) The dogs wanted in because it looked as is if might begin raining and they are scaredy-cats at heart. The cats were generally pissed because we had come home and disrupted their very important naps, but they were especially pissed because not only did we come home, but we let the dogs in as well.

Mom put a bookmark into her book and excused herself to the bathroom. I'm sure she had to go to the bathroom, but there was a part of me that figured she was just as pissed as the cats because we came home and disturbed her peace.

I began making dinner—like really making it; not just browning hamburger for some Helper. The girls finished their fight du jour and began working on homework between episodes of their favorite Netflix binge. Brian tapped out an angry email to the makers of the Two Dots app. The dogs settled in the corner and dozed. Aside from the cats hissing at the sleeping dogs, a quietness settled within our home.

I browned and crumbled the hamburger, tossing in some dehydrated onions and sprinkling some salt and pepper. (Fine! I was making Hamburger Helper—sometimes I need a helping hand, okay?!?)

My culinary pursuits (the mix doesn't open itself, y'all) were interrupted by my mom's shrill whistle.

Assuming she needed toilet paper, I stepped to the garage (where I hoard a few hundred packages of the two-ply) and grabbed a few rolls before heading back to her. Once in the bathroom, I set the toilet paper on top of the already full toilet paper holder. My mom was sitting on the toilet, fully clothed. *Fully clothed.*

Fully clothed? Of course, she was fully clothed. She's not one of those weirdos that has to strip down to nothing, *ala* George Costanza, to do her business. She's a stroke patient. That'd make each bathroom trip approximately forty-five minutes long.

What I mean to say is that she had her pants pulled up to her waist as any normal person would wear his or her pants (gang-bangers with their droopy drawers withstanding). She was sitting on the toilet with all of her clothes properly placed on her body.

"What are you doing?" I asked, hoping that she'd already gone to the bathroom, pulled up her pants and sat back down and didn't have a mess to clean up.

"Sitting here. Just wondering what I should do next," she answered very matter of factly.

I looked at her with a discerning eye. Was her face more drawn than normal? Was she having another stroke?

"Why are you wondering?" I coaxed. "Have you forgotten? What do you normally do when you've finished going to the bathroom?"

"Normally?" she began, "I sit in my wheelchair, then wash my hands, then return to the living room or my room or the kitchen ... wherever."

"Okay," I said, still mentally assessing her state of mind, "Why don't you do that?"

"Because my chair is gone."

It was then that I noticed that, indeed, her chair was gone. I was standing where her chair normally sat while she did her business.

"Where'd it go?" I asked turning a circle in the bathroom, as if the wheelchair would magically reappear after the second twist.

"I have no idea," my mom answered and she looked past me as if I were hiding it.

My mom is not stable on her feet, so she's always very conscientious about making sure her brakes, or wheel locks, are engaged before she stands from the chair. But, even if she hadn't secured the chair in its spot, where would it have rolled? The bathroom, like all rooms in the majority of homes, has a flat and level floor.

"Huh," I contemplated, still turning in circles. "I have no idea where it could be either," I agreed with her as I squatted down and looked under the cabinets, as if the wheelchair had not only folded itself up but had also shrunk itself, opened a cabinet door and hidden behind the Clorox wipes and super-sized bottle of Listerine.

So, I did the thing that seemed to come naturally. I yelled at Brian.

"Bubby! Where's Mom's chair?"

"What chair?"

What chair ... what chair does this man think is missing? Her recliner? Her dining-room chair? What chair indeed, dude.

"Her wheelchair," I hollered back without trying to hide the sarcasm.

"I didn't take it."

Well, at least we knew that he's not randomly taking items that his mother-in-law needs to function and selling them on the black market for more Two Dot apps.

Then, at last, I heard the telltale sound of rubber tires on ceramic tile.

"I hear it," my mom said in a whisper, so as to not scare away the chair.

"Me too," I whispered back and tilted my head toward the hallway from whence the sound came.

The front wheels of the chair appeared in the bathroom door, followed by the feet of Briley and eventually the rest of her and the missing chair.

"I love this chair!" she announced. "It's more fun than my scooter."

It's good to know that Briley is easily entertained.

Also? I told Briley to not take Nana's chair again—especially if Nana were on the toilet.

It's weird, the lessons I've had to teach my kids since Mom's moved in.

Weird But Improtant Lessons I've Had To Teach MY Children Since Nana Moved In

Nana's bed should not be left in the sitting-up position.

Nana doesn't want to watch anything animated, on Disney or involving a singing teenager; therefore, do not put those shows on her television and then leave the room with the remote.

The dogs are not allowed on Nana's bed, wheelchair or walker.

When replacing the toilet paper, the paper goes OVER otherwise it tears off one square at a time.

Also? REPLACE THE TOILET PAPER!

When Nana's showering, she doesn't want to have a conversation with you or listen to you sing.

Do not take Nana's food away from her until she's finished eating.

Nana's medicine container is not a maraca, a thing you toss or a spinner for a weird game of spin the bottle.

Nana's phone can receive texts; Nana doesn't know how to get to them though, so STOP IT!

Avocados Are Not Healthy

Gag-a-molé is what we call guacamole in my family. When we go to any one of the ~~dozens~~ ~~thousands~~ millions of Tex-Mex, Mexican, Hispanic, Latino restaurants that are located on every single corner of our town, we always ask them to leave the gag-a-mole off of our plate. If we're out with friends, we'll offer the gag-a-mole to one of them. And then when it comes to our table, and it's not in a completely separate bowl, we're likely to gag as we send the entire plate back. Also? I've been known to channel my inner nine-year-old and lie to the server and tell him or her that I am allergic. In a way, it's true. It makes me gag.

In a nutshell, we think gag-a-mole is gross. And disgusting. And disgustingly gross.

But my mom? She loves the stuff. She loves avocados and is always telling me that it's healthy and delicious. I tell her to shut up about it already because I'm *allergic.*

Since mom moved in though, fortunately for her, I made it a habit to buy three or four of the slimy green gross veggies during my weekly shopping trip. Unfortunately for me, it's not a smart move for my mom to use a knife, so I have to cut and prepare the avocado for her. This is usually done wearing a facemask and plastic gloves all while trying to not gag. In case I haven't been clear, I have a bona fide disdain for avocados. (Just typing the word gives me shivers.)

But, for my momma, I learned to deal. I also learned to prepare the avocado quickly and set it at the table as an appetizer of sorts so Mom could eat it before the rest of us sat down for dinner.

Now, it's normally an odd occurrence that we all get to sit down together as a family for dinner. Usually, I'm taking Hadley to golf or Science Olympiad or wherever, while Brian is running Briley to softball or basketball or pitching lessons. We'll all be home at different times and make our dinner plates at different times and, finally, all come together shortly before we fall into bed.

But on this particular night, we were all home for dinner. I can't even remember what I made, but I'm sure it was full of pasta, cheese and carbs to make everyone happy. And, for my momma, I decided to prepare a fresh avocado as a side.

The week before, I had dropped an avocado seed into the garbage disposal and spent about forty-five minutes digging that slippery sucker out with a pair of grilling tongs. I could have very easily stuck my hand down there and gotten it, but I was fearful of the disposal freakishly turning itself on and my ending up with a gnarled stump of a hand that would cause children and weak-hearted females to shriek in terror when I used the self-checkout line at Hellmart.

(Look how long that above sentence is—it's grammatically correct, too. Score one for grammar nerds!)

So, because I was fearful of a gnarled stump of a hand, I decided to stand over the trashcan and dispose of the seed.

I had half of an avocado in one hand and a very sharp knife in the other. I was pretending that I was on a cooking show, and I was narrating my actions in my head—or at least I hope it was in my head.

I had just made a pithy joke about preferring sharp cookies to sharp knives when I remembered watching a video on Facebook about seed tapping, or something like that; I wasn't really paying close attention. What I do remember is that you take a sharp knife and tap it into the seed and the seed will pop right out. I decided to give that method a whirl. I explained the technique (what I remembered of it) to my fake studio audience and then whacked the knife into the seed.

Only, it didn't go into the seed.

It went into my hand.

With the knife stuck in my palm, I had no choice but to drop not only the avocado into the trash but also the F-bomb like it was hot.

If I were really the star of a cooking show, we were going to have to edit the next few moments of this segment out before airing it. The FCC would never allow the language that spewed from my mouth to go on air.

The language that ejected from my mouth once I pulled the knife from my palm was not any better. It was, however, said in a much weaker and quieter voice because once the blood started flowing, I started feeling weak and quiet.

I stumbled from the trashcan to the sink and hollered for Briley to go get Brian. My mom, who had been sitting at the kitchen table reading, began wheeling her way over to me.

"What happened?" she asked, as I held my bleeding hand under the stream of water from the faucet.

"I stabbed myself with a knife. Do you have arteries in your palm?" I said, my voice starting to shake. "Briley!" I mustered up some strength to yell at my child, again, in the next room. "Go get your daddy!"

"Why?" she hollered back, probably not even moving her eyes from the television set.

*Let me stop my story here for a moment to wax poetic about the infernal question of *Why*. Why indeed, child. I know that the answer *Because I said so* will not suffice, but once—just one time—I'd like to have my child (either one of them) actually do what I have asked without my motives being questioned. Now ... back to my story.

"Because she said so!" my mom yelled at my daughter. I guess she's had to deal with kids asking her why as well. Must've been all of her dealings with my sister.

"Yeah," Briley answered back, "But why does she need him?"

"She stabbed herself in the hand, and she's bleeding!" my mom yelled. I'm not sure if it was my mom yelling or the fact that I was bleeding, but both kids, two cats, two dogs and one husband showed up in the kitchen.

After careful inspection by everyone but JJ the black lab, it was decided that I was going to need some professional, medical attention. We wrapped my hand in a towel after I gave last minute dinner instructions to Hadley, and then Brian and I started to leave.

"Heather," my mom called before I got all the way out of the door, "Where's the avocado?"

"It fell in the trash and probably has blood all over it," I answered, feeling woozy all over again.

"Well," she sighed, "we could probably dig it out and rinse it off..."

I shut the door behind me. I have no idea if she had an avocado for dinner that night.

P.S.—I know you're wondering, so I'll tell ya. We got partway to the emergency room, and I decided that I didn't really want two stitches, which is really all this particular cut would have required. It was deep to be sure, but long? Not so much. So, we went to the drug store and got some liquid bandage, pain reliever and some peanut butter cups, which is better than penicillin. All of this made me feel much better.

Nana Goes High Tech

I'm not really sure why we were in Owasso, a shopping mecca just south of us, but I know that we stopped at Sam's and ended up at Cracker Barrel. Now that I think about it, we might have gone just to pester my sister who didn't like for me to take our mom and her credit card shopping. I don't always need a good reason for doing what I do.

As we sat around the table waiting on our food and conversing, my mom said, "I think I'd like an iPhone." I believe she said this because we were, in fact, not conversing at all. Every other person at the table, aside from my mom, was checking her (or his) phone.

A few of us might have snickered at her. When I got done laughing at the thought of my mom with an iPhone (she can barely operate her flip phone—

and that was pre-stroke, y'all.), I explained that her phone plan would probably double in price.

"I also think the iPhone would be way too small for your taste. You need one that is at least double the size of the iPhone."

"Like an iPad?" she asked.

And that's how we ended up at the Apple Store after we ate our hash brown casserole and biscuits with honey.

My mom had wanted a tablet since I got my first not-so-smart phone many years before. She wanted to read books on a reader app. She wanted to check the weather and the news with just the tap of her finger. And she wanted to download the police scanner app and have that sucker going twenty-four seven. Crime never rests.

She had actually bought a tablet once—got a deal at the super-savings closeout store on a brand new tablet. She was so proud of her *Yeahright* tablet, and the name sounded Asian, so it had to be legit. Plus, she was only out twenty-five smackeroos if it didn't work out.

Guess what. It didn't work out. A touch tablet shouldn't have to be hammered with repeatedly with ones thumb in order for an app to open.

She was able to take it back and get store credit, with which she purchased one of those soaker hoses that shrinks to pocket sized when it's dry.

After that, she decided that she wanted a laptop instead of a tablet. So, I helped her pick out a laptop at Staples. I tried to convince her that a Macbook would last much longer and she tried to convince me that she wanted to shop local. After all, in order to go to the Mac store, we'd have to drive all the way to Tulsa, which we did about once a week anyway.

The problem with the laptop was that she didn't like it sitting on her lap. Also, it was mobile, and therefore, not as stable as a desktop. I know that these are surprising facts about a *laptop*, right? So, Brian and I bought her laptop (which promptly crashed), and we helped her pick out a desktop. She used this desktop religiously to like every page on Facebook and subscribe to dozens of email newsletters. Okay, that's not entirely fair. She subscribed to hundreds ... nay thousands of newsletters, each of which she printed out every time they popped into her inbox. This made cleaning out her office simply joyful, ya know, if you didn't mind recycling hundreds of bags of papers with thousands of recipes for a miracle smoothie that will make you lose weight with one swallow.

She would often call me from her office, complaining that the internet was broke or that Facebook was showing cuss words in her timeline without her consent. Then, she'd spend some time lamenting the fact that she couldn't watch *Law & Order SUV* or *S & M* (or whatever initials she was into) on her big television while sitting in her recliner because she didn't have a tablet.

After her stroke, during rehab, she sorely missed checking in with everyone on Facebook. I'd often take my MacBook or our iPad to The Village and take an us-ie (a selfie with more than one person, ya know), post a recovery report and let her scroll through her timeline. When she moved in with us, the first thing she asked for was her computer. We were way ahead of her though. We'd already moved it over and set it up for her.

But truthfully, for a left-handed person, the mouse is not a friendly device. Her therapists worked with her on learning how to use her left hand with special lighted mouse with a big, red scrolling ball. It was ridiculous and it wasn't that easy to use. I know because when my mom would end up with a gazillion windows open, I'd usually have to close them all.

Mom was frustrated with the desktop. I was frustrated with the desktop. When my mom would get on her computer, it would rarely end well.

So ... let's journey back to Cracker Barrel on that fateful night when she said she wanted an iPhone. To remind you: I told her that she couldn't have an iPhone on her plan and I was pretty certain that it was too small it would just frustrate her (and consequently me). And she said what about an iPad, and we went to the Apple store.

Knowing how my sister felt about spending money (she doesn't like it), I asked my mom hundreds of times if she were sure she wanted an iPad because I was sure that my sister would blame me if this whole purchase went south for whatever reason.

The Apple store is a whole family event, so my mom and I were in the van heading to the store, and the girls and Brian were in the SUV (not to be confused with the TV show).

"Can I skype on an iPad?" she asked.

"You can Facetime."

"Can I Facebook?" she continued.

"You bet."

"Can I get a police scanner?"

"You can have your pick of a dozen."

"Can I get recipes?" she asked, the excitement in her voice was tangible.

"There's an app for that, Mom."

"Can I read my Kindle books?"

"You have Kindle books?" I asked, incredulously.

"No, but you do. Can I listen to music?"

"I'll sign you up with my iTunes account."

"Will it have Josh Groban?"

I sighed, "We can download some."

"Can I Twitter?"

"You don't do Twitter, Mom."

Like a giddy school girl who was getting her back-to-school shoes, she asked, "Could I if I wanted to?"

"Probably not."

Our genius's name was Josh, like Josh Groban, my mom pointed out. He patiently showed us—all of us—an iPad and an iPad mini. Eventually, the girls and Brian wandered off and started messing with Garage Band and setting the backgrounds on the display macks to their wacky selfies taken with Photobooth.

My mom, Josh and I decided she'd really like an iPad mini—white—with a red case, no keyboard. We set it up as a device on my account, and I downloaded Josh Groban's self-titled album. We dragged the girls and Brian from the store and headed home.

But first, in the mall parking lot, we Facetime'd everyone we knew. My cousin Courtney finally answered and chatted with us for a while. Then, we did something horrible and unpleasant: We called my sister.

I'm not saying my sister was unhappy with our purchase, but she did report my mom's credit card and Mom's van as stolen with the highway patrol.

The Technology Learning Curve
in the Over 75 Set is
S T E E P
Like scaling Everest
When one is drunk
And has never scaled a
mountain before*

*This is actually a chapter about my mom's obsession with cooking, cookbooks, recipes, grocery shopping and all things culinary related. Also, I wrote the title and then closed out the document and now I don't remember where I was going with it other than everyday, my mom learns something new on the iPad and that makes me both happy and weary. My five-year-old niece, though, had already surpassed us both in her tablet knowledge. So, shift your paradigm right here. This isn't about my mom learning to iPad with the best of them. It's about her food-hoarding tendencies. But, it is a cool title, huh? I think I'll just keep it. Just don't get your hopes up about mountain scaling metaphors.

And now the real chapter: Currently untitled.

ееееееее

My mom was thrilled with her new toy. I gave her mini lessons, and my sister didn't speak to us for ~~weeks~~ ~~days~~ hours. Eventually, the only issue my mom seemed to have was when she had ninety-seven-hundred-thousand tabs open in Safari.

Occasionally, she'd "break Facebook." You were wondering who was causing all those issues with things from three years ago showing up in your timeline? It's all my mom's fault—or so she thought. I had to remind her ~~weekly~~ ~~daily~~ hourly that she just simply wasn't that powerful. Yet.

Not a day went by, though, that she didn't learn something new.

"Can I read the news?"

"Yep," I replied as I tapped the news icon and the news automatically appeared.

"Can I hear Josh Groban?"

"You bet. You can even watch him," I'd encourage her as I tapped the YouTube icon, blowing her mind and revving up her hormones. (Ewwwww, right? Was that too much to know about my 76-year-old momma? Maybe, but I don't care. This is my book.)

"Can I find recipes?"

Recipes. Ahhhhh ... she was looking for digital cookbooks. This could have disastrous consequences.

When my sister and I were growing up, my mom cooked on every day but Sunday. It wasn't that we strictly observed the Sabbath, it was that she was tired. She'd cooked all week long and felt she deserved a break. And honestly, she did deserve the break. So on Sundays, we'd have something easy at home, or donuts during Sunday School, Furr's Cafeteria Buffet for lunch and then, for supper, we'd have popcorn—the kind that you made with oil and a big ol' pan that you'd shake on the stove top. So, I guess she kinda did cook a little on Sunday.

But, her cooking didn't just start when she became a wife and mother.

She was born in 1938, the tail end of the depression. She was raised on a small farm, so they were fortunate enough to always have plenty to eat. In fact, they always had plenty to eat, not only for their family of six, but also for anyone else—family, neighbor or stranger—who happened to stop by. So, I imagine my mom, standing at the hips of her own mom and grandma, learned to cook early and plentifully. Like for an army.

When it was just the four of us, my mom, dad, sister and me, she would cook within reason with a few leftover servings for lunches. But, when she cooked for even just one additional person, say my sister and I had friends over or the neighbors came over, she cooked as though the Quartering Act were still in effect. Suffice it to say that if the 101st Airbornne were to stop by on any Independence Day or Memorial Day or Thursday, my mom could feed them all and send them each home with a Tupperware container of leftovers.

(For those of you who are not privileged enough to sleep with a social studies teacher, I'd like to pause and explain the Quartering Act. During our country's first few years in existence, we didn't have a military budget; therefore the room and board for a militia fell to the citizens and their homesteads. Probably, this would entail quartering—housing and feeding—no more than ten or so men at a time. My mother, however, translated this to mean that she would have to feed hundreds of our service men should they drop in.)

There were many evenings as a child that I remember my mom standing out on our front lawn and hollering across to our neighbor Sue and her two boys, "I'm making spaghetti! Come on over."

Then Chance, the neighbor two doors down would hear her and proclaim, "I like spaghetti."

And our neighbor Edith would step out of her house and say, "I've got some garlic bread."

Of course, my friend, Bobbi, would be over and I'd beg for her to stay and by the time we sat down in our tiny house in our tiny kitchen, there could be upwards of twenty people ready to eat.

The bonus of my mom's obsession with school-lunch-room style cooking was that she really did enjoy it. And one of her heartiest "hobbies" was born from this love of cooking—she collected cookbooks.

Once my sister and I moved out and the neighbors moved on, it was difficult for my mom to scale back her cooking for just my dad and her. Then, once my dad required full-time care from my mom, it was often times easier for her to take him out to eat. This did not stop her from buying cookbooks, making menus and going grocery shopping.

When my dad passed away, my mom found it very difficult to cook for just one. She continued to go out for her meals: Breakfast/brunch at Weezes and dinner wherever her taste buds led her. She also continued to buy cookbooks, create menus and shop for groceries.

Within one week into her rehab stint following her stroke, my sister and I knew we had to get into her pantry and fridge and freezer and clean those puppies out. Because, thanks to her Depression Era raising, she not only received the gift of cooking for the population of a Jersey suburb, she also received an attitude of "waste not, want not." And, well, let's just say she had enough Jell-O to build a three bedroom Jell-O box-walled home, and half of it was expired.

I'll bet you didn't know Jell-O expired. It does. Go ahead, go check the Jell-O boxes in your pantry. I'll wait.

See? Told ya.

So, while my mom learned how to stand again, my sister and I faced the daunting task of going through her food stash.

That which was expired, we trashed. I'm not even exaggerating when I say that we put out expired food for three weeks on trash day and took a truckload of expired food to the dump on free-dump day. The still-good, nonperishable food was donated, of course. When I took one grouping of it a local food pantry, they weighed in thirty pounds.

That was the most daunting task of clearing out my mom's home. Kinda. It was easy to do because my mom was not home.

Unfortunately, my sister and I didn't have enough time to get too much else done before she came to live with my family in July. And that meant that all those cookbooks that she'd been collecting, including the multiple (yes, multiple) cookbook clubs that she held memberships in, were still in the house when she came home to help us pack up her house.

The cabinet above the kitchen sink was full of cookbooks. She had four three-shelf bookshelves in the hall closet full of cookbooks. She had five baskets in the living room full of cookbooks. There were smatterings of cookbooks in all the other rooms as well, including the bathrooms. This doesn't even include the eleventy-thousand copies of internet recipes she'd printed out, ya know, in case the internet is ever discontinued and she can't find them again.

If I had to guess (and I bet it's a pretty good guess because I used to be an elementary school librarian), I'd say she had over five-hundred-billion-thousand-gajillion cookbooks. No hyperbole.

"I want to keep them all." She was resolute in her decision.

My sister, who has a five-year-old daughter and is used to dealing with difficult situations like this said, "NO WAY ARE WE KEEPING ALL OF THESE BECAUSE THIS IS RIDICULOUS AND STUPID AND I WANT TO BURN ALL THE COOKBOOKS BECAUSE I AM NOT LETTING YOU KEEP ANY OF THEM. NOT ONE SINGLE ONE, DO YOU HEAR ME?!!?"

I, on the other hand, who has patience that is only mirrored in the late saint, Mother Theresa, said, "Hey, let's work this out." Then I led us all in a soft and heartfelt chorus of "Let There Be Peace On Earth."

Between the three of us, we decided which cookbooks to keep (the ones our mom was a contributor to or had a personal connection with, such as church cookbooks or ones that had chocolate cake on the cover) and which cookbooks to donate (all the rest of them).

I consoled my mom by telling her that she could get a recipe for anything—*anything at all*—on the interwebz.

"Will you write down the password for me?" she asked as I loaded a box of cookbooks to put in storage.

"What password?"

"The password to get all the recipes," she replied.

"There's not a password. You can just go to a recipe site and find a recipe."

So ... when we got the iPad mini and I downloaded a few recipe apps, my mom was pretty much in heaven. Even though she didn't cook any more—she assisted—she enjoyed looking at the recipes.

And bonus for us: We haven't hooked her iPad up to a printer. This is a source of great sadness for my mom but a huge relief to trees the world over.

Crazy Cat Lady
or
"Heather, Come Get The Damn Cats!"

Brian grew up on a farm, so he always had cats roaming around outside. They were borderline feral cats. And they reproduced like, well, wild cats, so when one met up with a coyote looking for a midnight snack, there were always ten or so left in the barn to take its place.

I grew up with no cats. We had dogs but my parents were adamant that we were not to have cats. Since they both grew up on farms, I can only imagine that it was because they had lost too many precious feline friends to coyotes. That or they didn't want to have to care for them the same way they had to care for my dog. (I tried to remember to feed and water her every day. I tried!)

When Brian and I began the pet-adopting phase of our relationship, we got a puppy. Neither of us wanted cats. He didn't want a cat because he wasn't sure how you'd care for a cat in the house and, since we weren't living on a farm, he didn't want to have an outside cat. I didn't want cats because I didn't want something to happen to Brian and I be stuck with one cat and then I'd go get a new kitten because the cat and I were lonely and then while I was adopting the new kitten, there'd be an older cat who needed a home or he'd be let go to wander the big field in the sky, so I'd come home with fourteen cats and I'd smell like ammonia and I'd never leave the house and I'd learn to appreciate Friskies on Ritz Crackers as fine dining. (Mercy, y'all.)

Clearly, I had a cat-lady-phobia.

With our obvious disdain for cats, it was bound to happen that one of our daughters would want cats.

Hadley is a dog person. She likes our doggies. She wants to bring home every stray we encounter. She has never asked for cats one single time. And she's quick to remind us of this when they cats won't leave her bedroom.

Then there's Briley. It could very easily be because Hadley has made her love of all things canine known or it could be because I've verbally expressed my fear of becoming a cat lady, but Briley? She's the cat person in our family.

When she'd ask for cats, we'd tell her tales about litter boxes and shredded furniture and scratches and hairballs and cat puke.

Then, the dynamics of our neighborhood changed.

The Ranchers moved to town. The Ranchers had owned a cattle ranch operation and for reasons unbeknownst to even them, they sold the cattle and moved to town. They did, however, keep the horses and boarded them on a little bit of acreage south of town. On occasion they would bring in hay to feed the horses, but wouldn't exactly have time to take it to the horses so the bales of hay would sit in front of their house—directly across the street from our house—until they could head south of town and feed the horse.

Well, I was not raised on a farm, but I do know enough about hay to know that it's the Manhattan penthouse for mice. Therefore, when the hay sat in our front yard, the country mice went to town.

Unfortunately, we found ourselves infested with mice. We set traps. We bought those plug in electric things that are supposed to drive the mice crazy. We set out poison where neither kids nor dogs could get it. We even became proficient at throwing the television remote with just the right pitch and spin to actually hit and kill the brave mice who meandered into the middle of our living room floor while we were still awake.

One weekend after we had killed no less than a dozen mice, I asked a few of our neighbors how they were dealing. Weirdly enough, they hadn't had an ounce of trouble from the mice. Each of our conversations ended the same way. The neighbors would tell me that they owned a cat (or two) and I would hang my head and whimper.

The weekend we killed twenty-three mice, Brian and I decided to give in. Briley's birthday was coming up, so we would just give her a kitten for her birthday. We went to one of the local shelters and adopted two sweet little brothers. Briley named them Leonard and Sheldon after the beloved characters on *The Big Bang Theory*. We're nothing without our pop culture.

I sent Brian to do the bidding and pick up the kittens when the big day arrived. He'd been in touch with the shelter on several occasions and each time he reported that the median age of volunteer there was probably 92. He also reported that instead of cages, the cats were left to roam free in the facility. Sounds sweet, and I'm sure it is, but it makes for a couple of very skittish kittens when being introduced to children. Any children, nay any people other than full-grown and mature (as in AARP mature) adults cause great anxiety for the our new cats. This made the birthday party with twelve ten-year-old girls really fun as they chased the kittens under the couches, on top of the closets, and through the linens.

The birthday ended, and life settled down. The kittens turned into cats who turned into mousers. The mice disappeared from our home and the

Ranchers moved back to the country. (Of course. Isn't that the way it always works?)

But, we committed to the cats and they got to stay. And really? They haven't been half bad. For the most part, since tweens and teens are loud and unruly and (usually) anything but gracious, the cats have stayed hidden. They'll come out once the girls are in bed and love up on Brian and me. But mostly, they do their own thing, keeping the house rid of bugs, the occasional varmint and those pesky laser lights, and we do ours. I just always assumed they were unsocial animals.

Then my mom moved in.

These cats—these cats that would climb a lamp so they could leap into the top of the closet and hide behind some forgotten box of souvenir shot glasses every time they heard my niece's voice in the front yard—they became social, seductive animals to my mom. They rubbed her wheel chair; they climbed up her back and kneaded her head; they kissed her ears and elbows and audibly purred as if they were summoning the mother ship. They loved her.

And along with my mom came her therapists.

Most of her female therapists had long hair, and I swear I heard one of the cats say, "Hair? Praise Jesus!" before he began combing through it, tenderly, with his claws.

Thankfully, her therapists understood that home health care often meant dealing with the animals in the home. They were very understanding with the cats. My mom, however ... not so much.

"Heather? Come and get these cats!" she'd holler when the cats would begin to give the therapists a cat-tongue facial massage.

The therapists would often interject and say, "Now, we don't mind your cats, Harriett."

And my mom would reply, "They are not my cats."

Oh, but in a way they were.

When she'd yell for me to get the cats, I'd lock them in the bathroom and then we'd spend the rest of her therapy time listening to the cats cry. All too often, their cries sounded very human as I could make out the words *Let me out or I will cut you in your sleep, you weak human.*

Once they were let out, they'd make a bee-line for my mom's room and slather her with kisses, offering up their massages as a way of making amends for not being with her during her therapy. Again, I swear they could speak: *We are so sorry we were kidnapped and couldn't offer our services to you. Forgive us. Forgive us, please and let us rub your head in your sleep.*

Eventually, the therapy sessions ended and the cats had to go back to coming out at night when the girls were asleep. My mom still maintains they are not her cats, and I still vow to never become a crazy cat lady.

My mom, however, tells a different story. She says I've already become a crazy cat lady. But, I swear to you: Those cats have given me the best scalp massage I've ever had.

And if letting the cats massage my head makes me a crazy cat lady, well, then, pass the Ritz crackers and pop a top on some Friskies.

Not really.

Gross.

But, I do let them play with my hair.

Nana Gets All The Cool Things

Don't think that because I share all the fun and funny things about Mom merging with our household that everything was all roses and daffodils. It wasn't.

Hadley was a budding teenager. She'd had, however, the attitude of a thirteen-year-old since she was about four. And her favorite, *favorite*, *all-time-favorite* thing to say in a heated moment was, "I'm going to go live with Nana."

There were some days that Brian and I actually contemplated it. Even pulled out a suitcase to help her pack.

There were some days that Nana would have taken her.

Mostly, though, it was a safety net that Hadley fantasized about. When things were not going the way she expected them to go at our house, she could just transplant herself at Nana's home, where everything always went Hadley's way. #truth

So, Hadley really had a hard time with Nana's stroke. She was confused by what it meant for Nana. She was frustrated by the time I was spending with Nana, particularly during Nana's stay at The Village. In fact, one afternoon when I misunderstood our schedule and Hadley was late to an event because I was with my mom, Hadley told me that when I was in a nursing home, she would never come visit me because she would have better things to do. I told her that it was fine by me and at that exact moment, I meant it.

For Hadley, my mom's new normal was a transition she did not easily adjust to. So, when we talked to the girls about Nana living with us, Briley was game for it. In her little tween mind, it would be endless days of slumber party shenanigans. Hadley, however, wasn't sure about it. And once Mom became a part of our home, it was difficult to for Hadley to see her "Plan B" was no longer a viable option. On the days that she was especially aware of my mom's limited capacities, Hadley would shut herself in her room and blare Imagine Dragons while Instagraming moody selfies.

My mom, who still wanted very much for her oldest granddaughter to be a part of her life, would wheel by Hadley's room and knock, usually adding some silly comment. Hadley found no humor in this. It's hard enough being thirteen, but it's really hard when your Nana moves in and takes away your "escape plan."

But, eventually, Hadley (and Nana) came to terms with the new family dynamics and were able to regain their same sweet relationship, minus the midnight ice cream treats and hours of endless television watching.

Briley, on the other hand, well, this girl's cup is not only full, it's so full that it's bubbling over the edge endlessly. In fact, she doesn't have a cup; she has a fountain. She's a positive kid—she always has been and, hopefully, she always will be. Having her Nana move in was just one of the greatest things that ten year old had ever encountered.

Plus, Nana brought a lot of fun toys with her.

Before we proceed, let me be clear about the word "toys" in this instance. These are not the toys mentioned in the glossary of my second book, *Getting Lucky*.

At my mom's house, she had all kinds of toys. She had every single stuffed animal she'd ever laid eyes on. She had every single McGaggle's Super Extravagent Meal toy that had ever been produced since I went to college. She had all the books ever sold at any book fair. She had over a dozen boxes of crayons, markers and colored pencils. She had craft supplies and electronic games and all kinds of crap that kids seem to get a kick out of that my sister and I never had when we were kids. My mom had everything a kid could ever want.

That's not the kind of toys I'm talking about. To be completely honest, when my sister and I started cleaning out my mom's house, we kept a few sentimental toys (well, I did, anyway; my sister wanted to toss it all because her heart is made of a cold, marble slab). Mostly, though, we donated the toys. Our girls have plenty of toys at their homes and what joy could we bring to another child by donating my mom's toys! At least that's how we sold it to Mom.

So, what toys did Mom bring with her that caused great excitement for Briley? Well, let me just tell you about them.

First, my mom brought a hospital bed. This, according to Briley, is the coolest bed ever. You can just lay in the bed and use the remote and raise and lower your legs, your head and even your whole body. "How will Nana ever be able to sleep in this without playing?" Briley earnestly pondered.

My mom also brought with her a four-wheeled walker with a basket that doubles as a seat. Truthfully, it was an uneducated purchase for my sister and me. The brakes and wheels with just one working hand were actually too much for my mom to handle, but we bought it anyway. And not a day goes by that Briley doesn't give praise for our ill-thought purchase. We could take it back, but when we see that little tween pushing herself from the TV to the kitchen to the hallway and back again with such joy on her face? Well, who can deny the child that pleasure?

Mom also brought two hemi-walkers (half of a regular sized walker for use with just one hand) which are great to put together and pretend that you are doing the parallel bars in the Olympics (or so I've been told and have witnessed).

But the *piece de résistance* was the shower chair. The shower chair was designed to fit over the side of a tub, but since my mom was using our walk-in shower, we would just place it under the shower head and my mom would sit and slide to position herself for maximum cleanliness. When Mom's shower was done, I'd dry off the chair and place it in the hallway until she needed it again. The rest of us, well, we could just stand in the shower.

Except Briley.

Briley, who's a softball-playing studette, really wanted to try out the shower chair, but she'd always wait until I had it dried and put away before expressing her wishes to just give it a test run.

Then one day, as my mom was finishing her shower, I grabbed an extra towel from the cabinet and was startled by a booming yell, "Wait, Momma!"

When I was confident that I had my bladder and blood pressure under control again, I turned to face by baby girl.

"I wanna use the shower chair," she said as she stood in front of me, her hair in a top knot so it wouldn't get wet, a towel wrapped around her otherwise shower-ready body.

"Why?" I said, tired and wanting nothing more but to sit down and thumb through Pinterest.

"It just looks like something I'd like to try out."

I shrugged. Who can argue with a statement like that? I put the towel back in the cabinet and got out of her way.

That night, she took a forty-minute shower. She sang the entire score from *Mamma Mia*. She skipped to the living room smelling citrus-y and powdery and wearing clean pajamas (this is actually a big deal for her, y'all).

"That was the best shower I've ever had in my whole life," she sighed as she snuggled up next to me on the couch and drifted off to sleep.

Fast forward a couple of months. It's spring break and I have the stupid flu. It's official name is Influenza Type B, but I believe the "stupid flu" is more accurate. My body ached. My bones hurt, and I cried because I couldn't do anything else.

"Do you think a shower will make you feel better?" Brian offered.

"Maybe," I sobbed. "But I can't stand up for that long."

Enter the shower chair.

Brian positioned it and I dragged my poor, tired, weak self into the shower and let the water pour over me as I leaned back in the chair, enjoying the heat to my feverish body.

Almost thirty minutes later, Brian came in to check on me. "You doing okay?"

"Yes," I mumbled. "Just enjoying the best shower I've ever had."

Who knew the ten-year-old was onto something?

Oh. Em. Gee. Do NOT Mess With Criminal Minds

Prior to my mom's stroke, she had a total of five television sets: One in each of her three bedrooms, one in the living room and one on the back patio. Each of them was connected to cable television service. And the one in the living room had a DVD/VCR combo. I know that sounds very ancient, but consider the next sentence before you pass judgment. She also had about two hundred VHS tapes and movies. Now: That's ancient. The funny thing was she didn't watch any of them. She just liked having them around—kinda like the cookbooks.

(See a pattern here? Remember, friends, she's not a hoarder, though.)

At our house, we had one television set. It was in the living room. We had one computer, two iPads and each of us had our own smart phone, so really we don't need more than one television set. We had a DVD player, Netflix and a DVR. We are set.

When Mom came home, though, she needed her own TV. We could easily bring one from her house and have it connected to our service, so the cost was minimal. She could even have access to our DVR on her TV. This was a win in my book.

My mom, however, had never had a DVR; and, on more than one occasion, she had called me over to her house to fix her TV (read: turn it on). So, of course, it'd be something she'd have to learn and get used to, but I had confidence in her.

Our evening routine would be for the girls to go to bed, then my mom would go to bed and set her television to go off on its own in two hours, then we'd watch a few shows from the DVR and catch some late night funnies before we'd go to bed.

Right around the time Mom was discharged from The Village, Hadley discovered a little show called *Criminal Minds.* She also discovered a little station called "Criminal Minds All The Time Except When Cold Case Is On." For reasons which defy human comprehension, Hadley was watching her way through *Criminal Minds* starting with season one, episode one and recording all of the *Criminal Minds* episodes on the CMATTEWCCIO channel in whatever order they appeared.

Well, y'all, here's what you need to know about today's youth: They be cra-cra for *Criminal Minds*, and they also have zero tolerance for adult-folk who don't get technology.

Now remember when I told you that Hadley was having a hard time adjusting to a Nana who was not quite a good as new? Yeah, well, it didn't help matters when my mom's late night television viewing interfered with Hadley's constant recording of *Criminal Minds* on the CMATTEWCCIO channel.

The first I heard about it was one Saturday morning. I had heard my mom get up, use the restroom and return to her room. I squeezed my eyes closed extra tight so as to trick myself into sleeping longer. It worked.

Then I heard Hadley get up, use the restroom and go into the living room.

If you are thinking, "Man! She's got super sonic hearing," I'd like to also offer my psychic services to you right now as well. You are either a man or a non-mom. Because once one does become a momma, one is barely able to sleep because all the noises in all the neighborhood are amplified in a momma's head. So, in the wee hours of that Saturday morning (after nine o'clock in the a.m.), I did hear those things and was able to decipher, even in my tired and groggy state, exactly what everyone was doing.

So, after my mom was up and then back down again, and Hadley was up and starting her day, I was a little bit surprised to hear the *clomp, clomp, clomp* of my teenager's feet as they headed back down the hall and straight into my room. I squeezed my eyes shut and hoping she'd see me faux-sleeping and leave me alone, but the *clomp, clomp, clomp* of her feet told me otherwise.

"Momma!" she whisper-hissed, standing over me. (FYI—she had to walk right past her Daddy who had been snoring his fool-head off for the last nine hours and didn't whisper-hiss at him.) "Nana didn't record *Criminal Minds*."

I ignored her and faked a snore-snort to show her I was deep in sleep.

"Momma!" she whisper-hissed again. "Don't pretend to sleep, I see you squinting at me through your barely shut eyes. Wake up. This is a problem. Nana didn't record *Criminal Minds*."

"That's okay," I responded, keeping my eyes closed, without even squinting at her. "I don't think she wanted to record *Criminal Minds*."

"Well she didn't record it. And that's the problem. Get it?," she said louder. I thought for a moment that she would walk away from me since I clearly did not get it. Instead, she continued to hover over me like an FBI agent hovers over a victim's body.

"Get it, Momma?" she asked me again, her whisper-hiss turning into a growled command.

"Yeah," I lied, my eyes still closed. "I get it."

I didn't. I didn't get it. I had so many questions: *Did my mom want* Criminal Minds *recorded? Was*

my mom in the living room furious that Criminal
Minds *didn't record? Why was this my problem? Why
didn't my kids ever fix me breakfast in bed? Why
couldn't I just sleep until my body woke me up just
one time—one time??! Was this Criminal Minds
obsession a precursor to my own daughter becoming
an unsub or investigating an unsub? What does
unsub even mean? Why doesn't the FBI say perp?
Why don't they carry around those little* Blues Clues-*
like notebooks? What really happened to Steve on*
Blues Clues? *Is Hadley still standing beside me? Why
can't I ever just sleep in? I just want to sleep in. It's
my favorite. Sleeping ... it's my favorite ...*

"MOM!" This time, she was not using her inside
voice. Steve and Blue would be so disappointed.
"What are we going to do about it?"

"About what?" I asked, finally half-opening my
eyes.

"Nana messing up all the DVR recordings!"

All the DVR recordings? I hadn't seen *Modern
Family* from this week yet.

Fine, I was awake.

"Nana really doesn't even understand the DVR,
honey, so I'm sure she can't actually mess it up," I
explained as I stretched my way to a standing
position.

"Well," Hadley triumphantly explained right
back at me, "All of the *Criminal Minds* I had
recorded for last night are only recorded for one
minute. That's not even enough time for the credits
from the previously recorded show to stop playing.

I know you and Daddy wouldn't mess it up and it was during David Letterman's time slot, so who else could be doing it?"

"Maybe it's an unknown unsub," I countered, trying to save my mom from the wrath of the teen.

"That's redundant, Mom. Unsub means unknown suspect. You wouldn't say unknown unsub." I wasn't looking at her, but I heard her eyes roll ... this is just one of many of my Super-Momma powers.

The eye roll didn't bother me, though, because I was just thrilled to know what unsub meant. Bring on the FBI Crime Show Trivia Category. I could own it now.

So, still in our PJs, I began the investigation into the mysteriously not-recorded *Criminal Minds*. Sure enough, all the shows set to record during the David Letterman time slot had been interrupted. I explained to Hadley that Nana had never had a DVR before, so she really didn't understand how it worked. Then I promised to tutor Nana in all things DVR so that it would never happen again. Finally, I reminded Hadley that she had all of the episodes ever made on Netflix on her device, so I wasn't sure why this was such a big issue.

"I wouldn't expect you to understand, Momma."

"Well, then," I countered, prouder than I should have been, "expectation met!"

A few weeks passed, and I enlightened Mom to the fact that when any message popped up on her television while she was watching a show or changing a channel it would be best if she would holler for Brian or me. I started to have her holler for Hadley, but that's an awfully chancy holler—you never knew what you'd get in return when you hollered for Hadley or any other teenager as far as that goes.

I thought things were going just swimmingly.

Until I sat down one evening to watch *Modern Family*.

And there was only a minute recorded.

I removed the batteries from my mom's remote.

Just kidding.

Kinda.

We Don't Talk About Jack Sh!t

One late fall morning, as I was helping mom with her right sock and shoe, she said, "When I move out to Rachel's house ..."

The idyllic morning soundtrack that was playing in my head, featuring the songs of the Carpenters and John Denver, came to a record-scratching stop.

"What? When are you moving?" I asked her, feeling like I had failed as a home provider. Sure, maybe I should have done the dishes that one time I had to serve her drink in an empty prescription bottle because it was the only thing I had, but I thought I was resourceful. I thought our home had become my mom's home.

"Remember?" she said, oblivious to my shock at not being Martha Stewart. "We talked about this, *you*, *me* and *Rachel*."

Okay. So, let me just stop this little story right here and let you know how "we" talk about things, me, Mom and Rachel.

"We" usually talk about things while "I" am not around and then "they" say that "we" discussed it. But I'm here to tell you that half of the stuff that "we" talk about has never even made it to my ears.

Let me give you a few for instances.

Exhibit A: The Surgery.

Right after Brian and I were married but before we had children, I received a very huffy phone call from my sister.

"Thanks for not helping today or even checking in on us."

"You're welcome?" I asked completely surprised.

"Yeah, in case you were wondering, which I'm sure you're not, Mom made it through surgery just fine."

I gasped. "Wait. What? Surgery?"

"Yes," my sister said, obviously increasing her huffiness with every sentence. "She had a col-o-troup-o-scolono-optic-ectomy. We're home now. Doing fine. Ya know, in case you ever decide to care again."

"I had no idea!" I exclaimed. "Was this an emergency surgery?"

"No, Heather," Rachel sighed not even trying to mask her exasperation with her older sister, "*We* talked about it."

Exhibit B: The Executor.

One afternoon while driving home from school, prior to my mom's stroke (which I just now realized could have been abbreviated as PMS throughout this whole book and still have been sorta appropriate to the situation), my mom called and said, "Well, we went to the lawyer's office today." This was a little bit of a surprise because I had no idea she was involved in any litigation.

"She should have the papers written up for your sister to be executor of my estate when I'm gone."

"Oooooookay?" I responded, believing Mom already had those papers drawn up.

"You sound surprised. Are you okay?"

"Yeah, I just didn't know Rachel was going to be executor. I mean, I'm completely fine with it, but I just didn't know."

"Oh really?" she replied, it was now her turn to sound surprised, "Because *we* talked about it."

Exhibit C: The Move.

My mom began, "When I move to Rachel's ..."

I interrupted, "Wait, what?"

She explained, "Remember? *We* talked about it."

Yada Yada Yada.

Clearly, you can see that *we* talk about a lot of important things that don't seem to stick with *us*.

So, back to the story. Let me catch you up.

Mom said she was moving; I was shocked; she explained.

"I just don't want to become a burden on anyone, so we thought it would be best if I moved to Rachel and David's home for six months and then back with y'all for six months and so on. Remember? *We* talked about it."

Maybe they roofied me when *we* talk about stuff.

"Do you not want me to write this book?" I asked, speaking of this exact book that you are reading right now.

"The book is fine by me," she said. "I just know that your family is very busy, and I want you to have your space too. So I'll spend half the year with you and half the year with your sister. I'll get to spend time with their daughter and you can see me on weekends or when they go out of town, I'll come stay with you again."

"We're sharing custody?" I joked.

"Oh no. Rachel still has legal custody of me. Remember when *we* talked about that?"

ꙮꙮꙮꙮꙮꙮ

So, the plan was that mom would stay with us through the holidays and then move in with my sister and her family after the first of the year. My sister and I coordinated calendars so we'd know when mom would be at whose house during which events. We each wrote our arrangements on Mom's calendar, and we began the preparations for the transition from city home to country home. And when I say "we" in this paragraph, I mean all of us. I remembered that conversation. I also took my own lidded drink to the table. No one was going to roofie me this time.

Evacuate Nana, Part I

Stardate*: December 23
***I have no idea what Stardate means. I'm
trying to throw a little pop culture, Star Wars**
reference at you.**
****Fine! Star Wars/Star Trek. What's the
difference***.**
*****Okay, I concede. There's a big difference.**
**BIG PICTURE HERE, PEOPLE. The point I'm
trying to make with this whole "Evacuate Nana"
business is that it started on December 23, 2014
Just keep reading.**

The week before Christmas break, Briley woke
up not feeling great. As the morning quickly
progressed, she got worse: Her stomach ached, she
had the chills, and, generally speaking, she looked
really awful, even for a ten-year-old in the early

morning. Before we left for school, Briley had begun throwing up.

You know? I wouldn't wish a tummy bug on my worst enemy. But as sure as diarrhea follows vomiting, I wouldn't wish it on my mom. Especially when she was staying with me and couldn't quickly and easily maneuver to the bathroom, or anywhere else, for that matter. Since it was so close to Christmas break, Brian and I couldn't really miss school, so we left Briley home alone ... with my mom. But, I frantically called my sister and said, "Briley's home sick—GET MOM OUT OF THE HOUSE NOW!"

Before I go any farther, let me tell you a little something about my sister. She makes bona fide germaphobes look like dirty, commune-living hippies. If we have to sit in close quarters to each other (with or without anyone else), all I have to do is scratch my head, and she automatically believes she has lice. Sometimes I'll look at her and say she looks flushed, and she'll immediately get the chills and fear that she's contracted the flu. And when I'm feeling really rascally, I'll wad up a tissue and leave it where she can find it then tell her that I don't know where it came from. She'll Lysol the whole house while wearing a medical mask and sporting a double layer of latex gloves.

Truly, I have no idea where she gets her paranoia.

So, when I told her Briley was sick, and we didn't want Mom to get it so she had to evacuate her, I'm sure she grabbed a haz-mat suit before heading into town to ~~pick up~~ evacuate Mom.

I can only imagine how that scene played out:

Briley, who ended up having a quick-moving stomach virus, was probably lying on the couch watching endless episodes of Disney shows on Netflix. My mom was probably trying to get closer and closer and closer to Briley even though we had warned them both to stay clear of each other. My mom was maybe positioned at the end of the couch where Briley's feet lay. Briley was probably in a near-comotose state with *Wizards Of Waverly Place* playing *ad nauseum* on Netflix when my sister would ninja roll through the front door, wearing her haz-yellows and a gas mask. She probably pulled a drawer from my mom's dresser, dumping it in a red, plastic suitcase, resembling the hazardous waste disposal bins in hospitals. Then she probably wheeled mom out of the house while spraying disinfectant in her wake. She probably wouldn't even get close enough or slow down enough to ask Briley how she was feeling. But, that'd be okay because Briley probably wouldn't even notice that her Nana had left the house for at least four more episodes of wild, wacky, wizardly fun.

I wasn't there so I'm not exactly certain that's how it went down, but knowing my sister, I'd bet good money that I nailed the scene. If you ask her, though, she'd tell you that I exaggerate. Of course, you might not be able to understand what she's saying because she'd have a medical mask on.

Since our holiday plan was to leave two days later to go visit Brian's folks, Rachel just kept Mom at her house until we planned on returning on December 23. At that time, Mom would come back to our house until January 1 at which time, she'd go to Rachel's house to spend her six-month-sentence of hard time, or whatever, according to the plan I never officially talked about.

On December 21, I got a phone call from my cousin, Andy. He told me that his dad, my mom's brother, had passed away. His funeral was to be on December 24.

A Tale Of Quick Trips,
Not The Convenience Store

I'm offering you a little visual to refer to when you get lost reading the next two pages—because you need the visual because you will get lost. Each arrow represents a day. You're welcome.

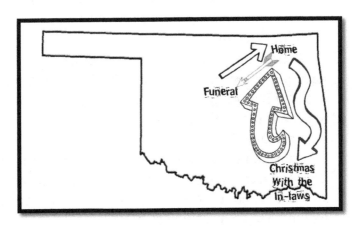

Briley recuperated fairly easily and quickly and we made our trip to Brian's folks down south. We planned to spend two days down there so that we could get back home in time to attend Uncle Norris's funeral. Since my sister had plans to spend Christmas Eve with her in-laws, she was going to bring mom back to our house on the morning of December 23. We would return home on the evening of that same day.

Sometime around noon, my aunt called and said she and the Texas family would be staying at a hotel the night before the funeral and they'd love to have us join them. I explained to her that we were traveling and I wasn't sure exactly what time we'd get back home, and while I appreciated the offer, I wasn't sure we'd be able to make it. The trip from my in-laws was a long four-hours if we didn't stop for restroom breaks. The trip to my uncle's home was an additional two hours in a totally different direction. It wasn't very likely that we'd make it to Stillwater that night.

Almost immediately after I hung up from Aunt Kay, my mom called. "Heather, Kay is getting a room in Stillwater. I think it'd be a good idea for us to get a room as well."

I explained to her that it would make for a very long day and we wouldn't get to Stillwater until well after ten o'clock and that it might be just as easy to stay home and wake up early to go to Stillwater as it would be to do any thing else.

"Okay, great." Mom responded, "I'll start packing."

I called Aunt Kay back and found out which hotel they were staying at.

I called the hotel and ask for a wheelchair and handicapped accessible room. (Oddly enough, there can be differences between wheelchair and handicapped accessible rooms.)

I called my mom back and told her we had reservations.

I called my aunt back and told her to expect us after ten-ish.

How in the world did we survive without cell phones? Or better yet: *How nice was life before cell phones?*

From the back seat, Hadley proclaimed that she'd just as soon stay home and go down the next day because she missed her own bed. Brian seconded her thought, so they made plans to come to Stillwater the next morning. Briley, before making up her mind, wanted a cast list. Who would be in Stillwater? Would her Texas cousins be there? Would she, too, get to stay in a hotel room? (P.S. Despite what it sounds like by her question, we've yet to make her sleep in the minivan while everyone else was in the hotel room.) And, would she get to go swimming? That last answer was a no, but she still opted to go with Nana and me that evening.

When we got home, I unpacked one set of suitcases and packed up another. I tossed my toiletries from our vehicle into my mom's vehicle. I kissed Brian and grabbed my mom's keys from the key hook and set off, with my mom and youngest daughter, in tow.

We got to Stillwater at about 10:30. Aunt Kay and one of the Texas cousins, L.J. were up waiting on us.

I got us checked in, unloaded the bags and scoped out the room. It had one king bed. It was decided that Briley would stay with Aunt Kay and L.J.. We visited for a little while, discussed continental breakfast plans, routes to the church in the morning and timelines for getting ready. Then Aunt Kay, L.J., and Briley went to their room where they ran the empty halls, knocked on closed doors and otherwise had a grand ol' sleepover.

My mom and I, however, went to sleep. We went fast to sleep and slept the sleep of royalty right up until my alarm went off at too-damn-early in the morning and my mom said she wanted to take a shower.

At this point in my mom's recovery, she was quite proficient at giving herself a shower in our shower at home. The shower in this room, however, presented a special kind of weirdness. It was a roll-in shower, but my mom didn't have a shower-proof wheelchair, so that was for naught. It had a hand-held shower nozzle, this was what we used at home, so it was perfect. It had a handrail that would enable to my mom to hold on if she needed it and it had a shower seat.

This sounds ideal, right? And right up until the shower seat it was ideal. The shower seat, though, my friends, it was not friendly to any of us. It was situated about four feet from the shower nozzle and the hand held nozzle had a hose of only thirty-six inches. The seat was also located about eighteen-inches from the floor. Even I wouldn't have been able to stand from the chair with any kind of success on a wet floor.

I'll give you a minute to do all the math. You'll eventually see that this adds up to a very good reason why even plumbers need algebra ... or at the very least math ... less still, common sense.

"I don't know how this is going to work, Mom," I explained as we stood looking at the sucky shower set up.

"Well, I still need a shower," she insisted. "Let's just make it work."

I sighed, stripped down to my underwear, stripped my mom down to her birthday suit and helped her walk to the bar, where she held on with her left hand, her back to the shower nozzle. I started the shower and then remembered that I didn't have an extra bra. I did not want to go bra-less and I didn't want to look as if I were lactating either, so I shed my bra and tossed it to the other side of the toilet. I did have another pair of panties, so if they were worse for the wear after the shower, then I could change.

Somewhere in the between washing my mom's arm pits and scrubbing her head as she stood naked holding onto the rail and I stood naked (partially) beside her, a weird thought occurred to me. If housekeeping or my aunt or any random person breaking into hotel rooms were to wander into this bathroom, we'd look very much like we were filming a super weird, highly-specialized, wild fetish of a geriatric /mid-life mother-daughter porn film. Luckily for us, no one came in.

Well, I say "luckily." I mean, if the price is right ...

What? *Pffffttt* ... I'm totally kidding. Totally. I mean, you cannot put a price on intimate moments with your mom when you are able to repay her in just a little way for the care she gave you to you as child. But, if you could put a price on it, it'd be six figures.

Scratch that: Seven figures.

My editor says that if I get that gig, I owe her a bigger chunk of change since she just had to read this chapter.

(*Editor's note: #Truth.)

Thoughts On Getting Older

My mom is 76-years old. She has two half brothers who were significantly older than she. In fact, they were closer to my grandmother's (their stepmother) age than they were to their half-siblings' ages. My mother's older brother is four years older than she is. Her younger brother is two years younger. And then the baby, my aunt Kay, is twelve years younger than my mom.

My grandfather died when my mom was sixteen. My grandmother (who was my Nana) died when I was seven. My mom's half brothers passed away before I really had a chance to know them. One died before I was born, and the other died about four or so years later. For the past almost-forty years, their family has been the four of them: Norris, Sissy (my mom), John and Kay.

And, like everyone else in the whole wide world, they are getting older.

But, until the past few years, they have seemed invincible.

My uncle Norris, the oldest of the four was diagnosed with cancer and battled the monster for a few years before moving from this life to the next in late December. It was his funeral that we all attended on that early morning on Christmas Eve.

My mom, Briley and I left the hotel and caravanned with my aunt Kay and the Texas cousins to the church to celebrate Uncle Norris's life. Brian and Hadley met up with us and the rest of the family there. All total, when we are all present and accounted for, there are forty-two crazy nuts on our family tree.

Having a stroke is difficult. Surviving a stroke is not only a blessing, but it also provides the survivor with lasting reminders of how quickly life can slip through your hands.

With my mom's older and seemingly impenetrable brother having died so quickly after her stroke, she was dealt a difficult blow. But she handled herself very well and grieved in her own way.

On the day we said goodbye to Norris, my mom showed her true strength.

My dad passed away just about thirteen years ago. The loss was something that I was upset about, sure, but I had been preparing for his death since his first heart attack when I was seven years old.

And, my faith allows me to believe that there's more to life than this world and that gives me great hope.

But, it was difficult looking at my mom grieving for her brother knowing that she was also staring her own mortality in the face.

Evacuating Nana, Part II: The Christmas Day Edition

We returned home after a very lovely service remembering Uncle Norris. We arrived home just in time to attend Christmas Eve Services at our church. Briley took great pleasure in telling all three hundred people at the services that night that it was "a Christmas miracle" that I didn't set my hair on fire. One little mishap with a candle during a very touching rendition of "Silent Night" and you've got yourself a Christmas Eve joke for life.

We left church, opened presents, put on our pajamas and promptly went to bed. All of us. Even the girls. This was uncharacteristic for them, but y'all? We were tired. We'd spent just as much time driving in the last couple of days as we had at our home.

My Christmas morning started off fairly normal. Brian was up earlier than should be humanly appropriate—he still thinks he's got cows to feed down on the farm. He stretched, grabbed the iPad and headed to his recliner to see if anything exciting had happened in the world since we fallen into bed the night before.

With the lights barely peeking into my bedroom window, I settled into a place where I wafted between dreams and the desire to empty my bladder. Then I heard it: smallish, socked feet shuffling down the tiled hall. I knew it was time for the frenzy of Christmas morning to begin.

Briley crawled into bed next to me, and Hadley plopped onto her daddy's pillow.

"Momma! It's not fair!" my older daughter lamented. "It's just not fair!"

To those experienced mommas and daddies out there, you know that at some point in the familial holiday celebration one of the kids is bound to cry that you clearly love the other child better because something that you've carefully thought out appears to be imbalanced in the eyes of that one child.

This was the first time, however, that the infraction had been publically blasted prior to the big present reveal.

The younger child gave a moan as her sister cried out about the injustices again, "It's totally not fair that she woke up with a fever and is sick on Christmas! I actually feel sorry for her."

Now they had my attention. First off, my baby had a fever. Secondly, her sister was championing on her behalf—this almost never happened.

I felt Briley's forehead; she was burning up hot. Then I felt my Hadley's forehead ... she felt normal. This was really weird.

I dragged myself from bed with an outraged big sister in the lead and a furnace-like child clinging to my waist.

Sadly and with great effort, the baby child opened her Christmas morning presents. Her sister only cried "not fair" once but quickly took it back when she noticed that her sickly sister was too weak to argue back.

Long story short (too late, right?), Briley spent Christmas morning (after opening presents, of course) with her fever moving higher and higher and higher until she landed in the Emergency Room, where she received yet another gift from the ER staff (how incredibly sweet was that?). She also received a diagnosis of the flu.

Since my sweet and ever-serving husband was up and dressed, he accompanied the sickly sister to the hospital, then to the pharmacy, then to the convenience store for some orange juice and 7-Up.

I was in charge of the big sister and the stroke patient, and my priority was to keep them (I mean *us*) from getting sick. First thing I did was call my sister. "FYI," I started when she finally answered the phone, "Briley's really sick again, so Mom's going to stay with you after dinner today."

"Wait," she said, the concern for our mother's health (along with my own health, I assume) was noticeably missing from her voice. "You're still coming out for dinner? Do you think y'all might have any germs with you? Would you be opposed to eating your dinner out on the patio and watching us open presents from the windows?"

I hung up on her and packed Mom's bags. Then, for good measure, I coughed into my hands and rubbed it all over Mom's suitcase. What my sister doesn't know won't kill her. Hopefully.

Our long-standing tradition is to not get dressed on Christmas Day, so Hadley was still in her pajamas when she, Nana and I loaded up the van and took off toward my sister's house.

We had a nice Christmas day, a lovely Christmas meal and had a great time opening presents. These presents included a child-sized drum set that I gave to myself but ask my niece to keep for me at her house. (I'm on a quest to earn the title of "World's Most Coolest Aunt" among the under thirteen set.)

But alas, it was time for us to go—I was about to fall asleep on my sister's couch and I was afraid that as I sat with my head tilted back on the sofa and my mouth agape, my sister would squirt Germ-X directly down my gullet. So, Hadley and I bade them all a Merry Christmas, loaded up our loot, and made our way home.

But wait. Would it be advisable for my girl and I—who felt entirely fine—to return home to the house of fevers and flu? I conversed with Brian and we decided that staying away might be to our advantage. We didn't want to spend all of Christmas break with a lousy-feeling kid or two or worse: a lousy-feeling adult.

To this end, I made hotel reservations, where Hadley and I ate dinner from the vending machine and binge-watched *Pretty Little Liars* on Netflix. At about three a.m., without knowing who A is, we turned in.

The next morning, we rolled out of bed barely in time to get a hard-as-a-reindeer's-hoof biscuit with a dollop of jelly-like gravy before we returned to the room to continue watching P.L.L., as we die-hard fans call it. When check-out time rolled around, we still didn't know who A was. But Brian reported that Briley was doing somewhat better, and he felt like it might be okay for us to come on home.

My mom, as a precaution, stayed out at Rachel's house for a couple of extra days just to make sure the flu bug was gone for good.

Then, just in time for New Year's Eve, we brought Mom back home. But only for two nights because after those two nights, she would be going to stay with Rachel for her allotted six months.

Christmas break of this particular year, was no break at all.

Moving Day
But, Really, It's More About Powder

Maybe it was denial that my mom was leaving. Maybe it was laziness due to the holiday. Or maybe it was absolute and sheer exhaustion because, gah! Being a momma and daughter and a wife and working full-time outside the home and writing a book and columns ... that's just hard, y'all. Just. Plain. Hard. It's so hard that when my sister showed up to take my mom to her house, I had not done one single bit of packing.

I told myself that if Rachel, like any shared-custody guardian, was so hot and fired up about taking mom from me then she could pack Mom up herself. I also told myself that it would be good therapy for my mom to pack up her own things and get her own self ready to move. And, I also told myself that I would never find out who A was in *Pretty Little Liars* if I spent my whole day packing and cleaning and taking care of my family. So, I pretty much sat on the couch watching Netflix all of New Year's Day.

And that's exactly where my sister found me when she came into town to get mom. It makes me yawn now, just thinking about how tired I was.

"Have you packed?" Rachel asked walking in, past my mom's room and pushing my feet off of my couch so she could sit down.

"I'm not going anywhere," I said, putting my feet on her lap.

"Obviously," she responded to my stained T-shirt and yoga pants and mascara goop clumped in the corner of my eyes.

"I have a few boxes," I offered. "They're in the garage if you wanna go get them."

"Geez, Heather," my sister rolled her eyes, "I'm not moving everything."

Then she proceeded to pack up everything. She didn't use any of my boxes, and I had to recycle them later on.

Like in March.

Because *why rush* was my New Year's resolution.

And in a matter of a minute or forty-five, my sister had packed up all of my mom's clothes, bags, books, computer, television set, medicine, cups, shoes, pillows, art work, fine wine, hidden candy, my hidden candy, her iPad, magazines, glue sticks and body powder.

I'll be honest here: The body powder leaving the house bothered me. It bothered me a lot.

My mom had always used body powder after she bathed. But, in the hospital and rehab, powder was contraband. It was such contraband that when my bae, Misti, sent my mom some of her favorite dry shampoo, we had to smuggle it in and use it outside on the patio. Because, y'all know, dry shampoo is nothing but aerosol'd powder.

Now I'm not entirely sure why powder—regardless of its aerosal'd or puffed forms—is such a bad thing. Maybe because it gets accidently snorted by former coke heads with "old-timer's disease." Or maybe confused residents put it in their coffee at five-thirty in the morning, causing the coffee to become paste that seals up their already-sealed-up intestines. I don't know. I don't know why my mom couldn't have powder in The Village, but she couldn't.

So, just before she came home, I went to Hellmart to grab a tub of powder with a great big powder puff. She missed that smell-good dryness it offered her freshly showered body.

Good heavens! Why am I not writing erotica? It's one of the most lucrative genres in the literary world. But let's be clear: If I were to write erotica, it would *not* be about my mom and her sadness from missing her body powder.

And speaking of body powder, we now return to our regularly scheduled story, sponsored in part by "Where the hell can you even buy powder with a puff anymore?"

When we left the story for our slight detour into quasi-powder-erotica, I was scouring the aisles of Hellmart for powder with a puff. You know where I found it? On the same aisle as unicorn food and make your own rainbow kits.

For those of you who missed my sarcasm, I didn't find any powder with a great big powder puff.

I found baby powder, which smelled so good that I actually felt myself ovulate right there in the baby section of Hellmart. I might have even whimpered a little bit and cradled my not-even-remotely-pregnant-but-looks-like-it-on-most-days belly. I couldn't bring home baby powder—I didn't want to start lactating every time my mom got out of the shower.

I couldn't get Gold Bond Powder because the television commercials freak me out. Powder can't cure fungus and stuff.

I found some Burt's Bee's Dusting Powder. But I wasn't really clear on how honey bees could make powder, and I felt like I was being taken for a fool.

And I found some weird-brand powder that claimed to be both organic and vegan. My mom was no hippy, so I passed.

So, I grabbed some Monkey Butt Powder (it's a thing, really it is) and headed home. For the next almost-six months, I would help my mom powder herself after her shower by putting a little Monkey Butt onto a washrag and dabbing it all over. It wasn't a powder puff, but it was the only thing I could find.

Apparently, sometime between my junior year in high school and my forty-fourth birthday, powder puffs disappeared from the aisles of Hellmart.

Then, I remembered that I usually bought my mom powder-puff-y things at Christmas. I'd start looking for the tubs of powder with the puff as soon as they put the holiday gift items out. In September. Right after Labor Day.

No sooner had the pool toys and vinyl picnic table clothes been put on the clearance aisle, than the gift sets began adorning the Hellmart aisles. But, guess what was glaringly missing? That's right, powder with puffs. There were no cheap, plastic tubs half-filled with powder and with one great big puff with a little pink ribbon on top all for $2.99. They were nowhere to be found.

Finally, when complaining to a friend about the lack of powder puffs to be found, she suggested that I go to the mall and check out the department stores. Eureka! I struck gold—powdered gold, that is. And for $65 plus tax (and no free gift with purchase, which made me feel completely gipped), I got my dear ol' momma a powder puff and a tub of very expensive, very lovely, very silky powder.

I remember the exact day I bought it—December 21. I gave it to her for Christmas. One week later, my sister came and stole the powder (and our mom).

So, this was how I started the New Year. A hole in my mom's room, a hole in my heart, and a hole in the bathroom cabinet where my mom's powder used to sit. Ya know ... for the last six days.

A few weeks later, I was packing up the remainder of my mom's house (read next chapter to find out exactly how that went), I discovered that my mom had not one, not two but three tubs of powder in her bathroom—all of them with powder puffs.

A Word Problem

If a 44-year-old woman and her 40-year-old sister cannot remember the exact date that their mother moved from one of their homes to the other and their respective spouses and children cannot recall the exact dates either, but their mother can open up her calendar and give the precise date of her moving from one dwelling to another, which one of these persons is the stroke patient?

Hint: It's the one who's seemingly got it all together.

"God took six days
to create the world,
but I can pack that house
in three days."

My sister, because she doesn't work outside of her home, took on the majority of cleaning up and packing up the rest of my mom's house. Now that my mom was with my sister full-time, the process had slowed down significantly. One Sunday afternoon as I was at my sister's home ~~eating her Little Debbie snack cakes and drinking her Grape Crush sodas~~ visiting, my sister mentioned that she just didn't know how we were going to get my mom's home packed up, cleaned out and ready to sell.

"We're going to need some help," my mom said very solemnly.

"I can get that house packed up within a week," I bragged. Wait. It's not bragging if it's the truth, is it?

My sister snorted, mumbled something about my being full of crap and snorted again.

"I can!" I exclaimed. "In fact, I can get it packed up *before* the end of the week." I sounded like a contestant on *Name That Tune*.

My mom took a deep breath, "Well, don't get rid of anything important and be sure to pack things so they won't break in storage and don't just donate things to the first place that's open; give it away to organizations who can use it. And I want to keep that one book shelf but not the other and see if someone is interested in buying the Neil Diamond eight-tracks before you donate them to a local school's music department."

I nodded my head and tapped the notes furiously into my phone. Really, though, I was texting my sister: Keep her away from the house for three days, and I'll be done by Wednesday.

(I don't know how we were ever sneaky before we had cell phones.)

My sister glanced at me and then rolled her eyes. To be honest, I couldn't exactly see her rolling her eyes, but I felt it. We're connected like that.

Monday after school, Brian took charge of the girls. They hadn't yet started golf or softball, so basically he just got them home and made sure they didn't fight over who got the iPad and who got the Macbook. I went to my mom's house. We had been collecting boxes for her home since she'd had her stroke. Additionally, she had approximately twelve dozen hundred Rubbermaid-esque containers that we could use stashed throughout her house. (Why? One word: hoarder. Don't tell her I said that.)

I started in the back bathroom. When I finished digging through the shelves and cabinets back there, I moved to her bedroom. And then the closet. And the next bedroom. And the linen closet. It's amazing how quickly a task can be tackled when one doesn't have the distraction of children, pessimistic sisters and hoarding mothers.

As I made my way through her house, I piled the boxes in two separate places, which were already established by my sister. (She made we type that.) Under the kitchen windows, I stacked the stuff to go into storage—this was the stuff we'd keep: Old yearbooks, pictures, graduation announcements, family Bibles, jewelry boxes, name tags from our first jobs, summer clothes, ya know ... that stuff that would mean something to someone someday. I was certain that *someone* would not be my sister and that *someday* would not be any day soon, but we'd keep it because it needed to be kept.

The other pile under the living room windows was stuff that we'd give away. This was stuff like the ninety-seven packages of colored pipe cleaners and the nine-and-a-half-years' worth of *Women's*

Circle magazines (with select recipes for the perfect pot roast cut out and placed in the appropriate shoe box, of course). Also in this pile was the Neil Diamond eight-track tape, the *Jazz Piano for One Hand* (book one), three sets of shower curtain rings, two bags of craft shells (made in China) and a random assortment of plastic (not silk) flowers.

My editor, Mari Farthing, has a gift for being able to name that tune with just the opening chord. I do not have this gift. Instead, I have the gift of packing up a house (save the seventy-three cleaning items under her kitchen sink) in just a day.

I'll say it again because it bears repeating if for no other reason than to irritate my sister: I packed my mom's house in one day.

Rachel here: She lies. It took her longer than a day, but she'll never admit it.

All that was left to do before we listed it with the realtor was to move the fridge, sell the furniture, clean off the back porch, clean out the storage shed, clean out the garage, empty the attic, cut the trees, and have the house deep cleaned. But what's important here is that I packed my mom's house* in one day.

*It should be noted that my sister and I (mainly my sister**) spent a great deal of time and effort prior to this amazing, one-day feat getting the house readied for packing. If you wanna know exactly what all we did—namely my sister—you'll have to con her into writing her own book. Or look for the crazy woman protesting my events carrying her sign that reads, "Hell No, She Is Not Solidly Responsible For The Whole One-Day Packing Fiasco!"

**The garage and the back porch and moving the fridge was all my sister and brother-in-law. They asked me to help, but I was wearing my "I Packed My Mom's House In One Day" shirt and didn't want to get it dirty.

Garth Brooks Is Always Worth The Wait

Garth Brooks, who is practically a neighbor, and his lovely wife Trisha, who once communicated with me on Facebook, were bringing their concert to Tulsa, just an hour from us. The tickets went on sale right before Christmas and since I was in the throes of Christmas shopping, we opted to not get tickets for ourselves.

I asked Brian if he thought his sister and brother-in-law, Lori and Jared, would like the tickets. He said he thought they would. So, I spent the better part of one morning with a half-dozen browsers open on my computer attempting to get tickets. He added a show or two and all of a sudden, I was offered tickets. I didn't even look to see where they were before clicking the "BUY THEM RIGHT NOW!" link.

We got the tickets (in the mezzanine area behind the stage) and then Brian said, "I'm not sure they'll like the concert." And long story short, we had ourselves two tickets to the Saturday night ten o'clock show the second Saturday of January. My mom agreed to spend the night with the girls since we probably wouldn't get home until well after midnight.

Hadley had just turned thirteen. She was finally an official teenager. She had been babysitting for various people for about a year and the idea that her grandmother was going to come over and spend the night like a *babysitter* kinda made Hadley feel like a baby.

"If other people trust me with their kids, shouldn't you trust me with your kid?" she argued with me one morning on the way to school.

The part of me that still saw her as a waddling toddler singing Barney songs wanted to scream that I didn't trust her or anyone else to keep an eye on my precious kiddos, herself included. (Did you follow that? It makes sense in my head.)

But another part of me wanted to offer her this chance to prove herself as a maturing, trustworthy young adult. So, I called my mom and told her that she wouldn't be needed the girls would be fine by themselves. She screamed into the phone that she didn't trust me or anyone else to keep an eye on her precious granddaughters.

I hung my head in almost-defeat. I understood how she felt.

So, I texted my friend Jennifer and ask her to be on stand-by in case of an emergency since we'd be far, far, far away (like fifty miles) and out late (like after eleven).

Jennifer texted back that she'd gladly do that. She also thanked me for not accidently sexting her, but that's another book. (Have you read *Getting Lucky* yet? You should)

The night of the big concert, I got the girls a frozen pizza and told them to keep the door locked. I shared with them the neighbor's phone numbers and made sure their phones were charged. I called The National Weather Service and asked for a minute-by-minute prediction of the weather in our exact longitude and latitude. When all looked like it was good for us to go, we left.

Brian and I enjoyed dinner out in the big city. We'd taken advantage of our girls' growing independence on several occasions for dinner in our own town. But, we were going an hour away. There were more possibilities. There was an Olive Garden, y'all.

After eating our meal without referee'ing any quarrels, sopping up spilled drinks or apologizing to fellow diners for the sibling-arguing gone wild, we made our way downtown, tickets secured in our coat pockets and stood in line on the coldest, windiest night of the winter thus far with about fifteen-thousand of our closest friends, waiting for the 7:15 show to release so they could let us in for the 10:15 show. At almost eleven o'clock, the crowds began exiting.

I texted the girls and told them the first concert was just ending and we were still waiting to get into the venue.

We got to our seats at almost midnight. I texted the girls and told them the concert still hadn't started, so we'd be late in getting home.

At a little after midnight, Garth took the stage, and I texted no one because OHMYGOSHGARTHBROOKSISON!

For a little over three hours, I was reminded of several things:

1. Garth is totally deserving of the title "Entertainer of the Year."
2. I love Trisha Yearwood, and I still have a burning desire to cook with her.
3. I know every single lyric to every single Garth Brooks song—and then some.
4. "The River," "The Dance" and "You Move Me" make me cry.
5. It might be physically impossible to not throw your arms over your neighbors' shoulders and sway while singing "Friends In Low Places."

The concert ended and hand-in-hand, Brian and I walked to our car. I may or may not have serenaded him with "Shameless" on our trek there.

(Fine, I shamelessly sang it and sang it loud.) When we pulled from the parking garage, I glanced at the radio and wondered why they weren't playing non-stop Garth songs so that we could reemerge easily from the concert. Then I noticed the time. It was well after three.

I checked my phone. No one had called or texted. I took that as a good sign, but the nervous momma in me took right over for the star-crossed music lover in me. I checked our neighbors' Facebook pages. None of them mentioned cops, ambulances, fire trucks, earthquakes, robberies, convict escapees or sink holes. I was going to assume that the girls had just fallen asleep while sneaking in an episode of *Saturday Night Live*; I imagined that every light in the house would be on.

We pulled into the driveway slightly before five and, just like I suspected, the house was lit up as if we were trying to communicate with the space station. I sighed a contended sigh. They were growing up. Technically, they had just spent the night by themselves and had seemingly survived. They were growing up and their need for me and their daddy was waning. If we weren't careful, we were going to blink and they'd be moving out on their own.

Maybe it was because I was tired (probably it was). Maybe it was because my mom had just moved out two weeks prior. Maybe it was because the certainty of my babies growing up had just been proven. Maybe it was just Garth and Trisha.

Whatever the reason was, I was overcome with emotion. And I had to choke back sobs before I could exit the vehicle; I had to get myself and my emotions under control before I walked into our house. I was verklempt as my Yiddish-speaking friends are wont to say.

(P.S.—I have no Yiddish-speaking friends. If you speak Yiddish and would like to be my friend, email me!)

Hadley was asleep in the recliner. Briley, with noticeably dark circles under her eyes, was sitting on the couch. "Oh good," she sighed, visibly relieved at the sight of us, "You're home. Hadley told me that on *Criminal Minds* sometimes when parents were out, they were killed and the FBI had to come tell the kids they were dead, so I've been waiting up in case someone knocked on the door I wouldn't miss it."

So ... we had a little bit more time before this one was ready to be rid of us.

And ... I really enjoyed my night out with my lover without worrying (too much) about taking care of anyone else.

lllllllll

Pretty much, this night sums up the sandwich generation. It's hard to balance the gentle task of letting go of our children and holding on to our parents while trying to live our own lives. Balance? Pffffft. It's unachievable.

But ... we do what we can. And usually, at the end of the day, we'll find ourselves with our hands full—that's a good thing because one day we'll find ourselves with both hands empty.

And in the immortal words of Forrest Gump: That's all I have to say about that.

End of sap.

And Now For Some Q & A

A little more than a year ago, I had no idea how different our lives would become. I use the pronoun *our* instead of *my* because, even if I were the only one caring for Mom, everyone's life would be impacted. Thank goodness, though, I am not the only one in this.

First, let me be clear on this point: I am fully aware—and offer my thanks in my daily prayers—that my mom has the faculties and abilities that she does. I have friends, old and new, who are in situations with parents who are physically able but mentally or intellectually unable to care for themselves. I have friends who are in situations where they are not able to offer the care their parents need and have to allow others to take care of them. I have friends who have since said goodbye to parents after caring for them. We all have our own crosses to bear and none of those crosses are the same. This makes life beautiful and burdensome all at the same time.

I've spoken with various caregiver groups since my mom's stroke. Because I'm writing this book and have written several other books, this gives me the appearance of being an expert in this field. Just so we're on the same page: The only thing I'm truly an expert on is sleeping in. I can sleep in better than anyone else I know. In fact, I even trained my kids to sleep in. #truth (It worked for one kid and kinda, sorta, not very well with that other—she gets it from her daddy.)

I do like speaking with these groups, though. I like hearing their stories and, as I've said before, even though their situations and stories are completely different than mine, I like knowing that I'm not alone in this plight. In fact, I'm even sure that my sister would tell a drastically different story than I've told in this. (But, you'll have to convince her to write her own story if you want to hear it.)

So, I thought it'd be good to share with you some of the most-asked questions (and my answers) here.

How do you and your sister work so well together?

Good question. We work well together because I tell her what to do, and she does it.

Not really.

But kinda.

A lot of real experts will tell you that it's important to keep the lines of communication open between all family members and can I just get an *Amen* for unlimited texting plans? We don't have meetings, but we do communicate frequently albeit informally. Just last weekend, I was at my sister's home and we went to feed the horses across from my sister's house. My mom was still on the patio because the country road was wet from spring rains. While we were feeding the horses whole apples, we chatted about my mom's lack of exercise. We can't have this conversation necessarily in front of mom because she lies about exercising. So, we find the best times and places in order for us to talk about my mom's care. And last weekend, the best time and place was standing at the field where the horses gagged and threw up whole apples. (Note to self: Cut the apples next time.)

Who makes the decisions, you, your sister or your mom?

It's me ... allllllllllll me. Have you ever done any research on birth order? I am the oldest girl. My mom is the fourth born to her dad and second born to her mom; she's the first girl. I have no idea what that means in terms of birth order. I guess that's just trivia. My sister is the baby. Clearly, I am the only one who has the naturally-ingrained skill sets that allow me to make the best decisions for our situations. But, we have a checks and balance system in place. And that is that my sister does whatever she wants to anyway (see also *last born child*). My mom's just so thrilled that we sprung her from The Village where she doesn't have to hear Ruby cuss out the nurses aides and call my mom the b-word, that she doesn't care what we decide. So, who makes the decisions? I think we all think we do, but truth be told, I'm not really sure that any of us is the official decision maker. Except me. It's alllllllll me. And sometimes Aunt Kay.

Who makes the rules, you or your mom?

When I was twenty-one years old, my mom was of the opinion that she could make the rules in her own house. In fact, the details escape me, but I recall a situation the summer I turned twenty-one and was home from college wherein she said, "A castle can have only one queen and this is *my* castle." Again, the details are fuzzy, but I think her point was that she was in charge. I am now forty-four years old, and I take great delight in throwing that quote back at my mom at least once a day. Not always aloud. Sometimes I say it under my breath as I stand behind my bedroom door, but I still say it. I wouldn't dare say it to my mom's face though, because, well, she is the queen.

Do you go to a support group?

Once a week, I meet with three of my good friends and we critique each other's writing. Sometimes I put my head down on Marilyn's Ethan Allen dining room table and sleep, and they support my desire for late evening naps, so I guess technically I do have a support group. They aren't a support group for caregivers because they have different situations than I do. But, they don't go to a support group for moms of three year olds or a support group for moms who are planning two weddings in one summer or a support group for raising a diva. I could go to a caregiver support group, but I find that my friends—particularly Christine, Jennifer and Marilyn—support me nonetheless. I meet with my friend Dawn almost daily and just dish on life in general. I meet with Brian every night when we lay in bed and discuss the day that has passed and the day that is to come. I text with Misti and Julie about whatever crosses our minds whenever it crosses them. And, of course, my sister and I discuss things pertinent to my mom when we need to. I have support even though it's not through a designated caregiver support group. I have nothing against them, it's just that I don't need that support at this point in time.

Would you be willing to start a support group?

If by starting a support group, you mean meeting with friends at the Embassy Suites and pretend that we are hotel guests to get free Amaretto Sours during happy hour, then sure! I'm game.

How do you keep your sense of humor about you during tough situations?

Wait. I'm funny? Good to know.

Having a sense of humor is something that my mom passed on to my sister and I at a very early age. Laughter can be found in every situation. She won't admit it, but I'm pretty sure that when Brian and I were kissing during our wedding ceremony, it was my mom who yelled, "Get a room!" I recall a time when my mom woke us up as she was watching a *WKRP in Cincinnati* episode to share with us the saga of the phone cops. She laughs about getting stuck in the laundry room. She laughs about spending money at the super-duper shopping club. (My sister doesn't laugh about that, though.) And I'm sure she'll laugh about this book. So, my sense of humor? It's all my mom.

Does your mom know that you're writing about potty training her?

Okay, so here's the deal. In the book I give her, I've redacted certain parts with a black Sharpie. So, let's just keep that little secret to ourselves, mmmkay?

When do you find the time to write about your experiences?

I'd love to discuss my time management system with you, but call before you come over so that I can pick up the living room and find a clean pair of underwear to put on. Also, please bring us something to eat because I cannot recall the last time I actually went to the grocery store. So, if you don't mind a messy home with a stinky, out-of-shape host and nothing to eat, I'll gladly meet with you from 3:15 to 4:30 on Sunday mornings because that's the only free time I have.

What does your husband think about having his mother-in-law live with him?

I am not lying when I say that having her move in with us was Brian's idea.

Brian here: She's not lying; it was my idea.

I am also not lying when I say that there have been some adjustments. Finding the best time to be intimate has been a thinker.

Brian here: She's still not lying.

When we bought our house, we joked that the little eight-by-eight room off of the laundry room would be a great place to keep mom when "the time came." Actually, it's turned into a room where our dogs stay when it's raining. (Our dogs are wimps.) It looks like dogs live in it. It smells like dogs live in it as well. Brian has always joked that Mom could live in that room for as long as she wanted.

Don't think badly about Brian, though. My brother-in-law said Mom could live in the well house. At least our room is vented.

So, I think the fact that my sister and I have very supportive husbands is probably the number one factor that our arrangement works.

Brian here: She doesn't actually live in the dog room.

Have you had to sacrifice your family time with this change in your lifestyle?

The truth is this: I probably have. The truth is also this: My family lives a very full life. Hadley is active in publications (she takes after her momma), participates in Science Olympiad, takes all honors or advanced courses, plays golf for the junior varsity team and is a budding photographer. Check her out on Instagram (@seasons.inspired). Briley is a competitive softball pitcher. I'm not good with numbers, but she's had a lot more strike outs that she has walks. She also likes to sing and is active in our church. Brian gives softball lessons in addition to teaching full-time. The word sacrifice means to offer up or give up. We've not done that at all. If anything, we've sacrificed nutrition because more times than not, we eat take out food. It's not perfect, but it's our life. Plus, the people at McGaggles already know what we want and when we want it, so they really are saving us time having our order ready to go before we actually drive through.

Would you do it the same way again?

If ever there were a stroke prevention pill invented, I'd go back and give my mom that (my dad, too, as far as that goes.) But, until that time, I wouldn't do anything any differently. Except maybe I'd sit with Ruby at The Village and cuss just because I could.

Acknowledgements

Or
I love these people
and can't not mention them
at least once, if not twice,
in every book that I write

First off, I'd like to thank my own momma, Harriett, for having a stroke. If it weren't for her health issues, you'd be reading a book full of blank pages right now.

JUST KIDDING! I wish my mom had never had a stroke. I wish that my Disney Death could have been an absolute truth for her. But it wasn't. I'm not grateful for my mom's stroke. I am grateful, though, that my mom allowed me to tell our story with humor and honesty. Just for that, I'm going to give her an extra bottle of Febreeze for her dog room.

Again, just kidding. She doesn't live there. The dogs would never tolerate that.

My sister, Rachel, will probably never read this book, so I'd like to take this time to publicly apologize for several things. I'm sorry that I took you to get your hair cut when you were thirteen, which resulted in the era known as "The Very White Girl With The Big Afro." Okay, that's enough.

But, I'm grateful for her and her devotion to our mom. She gives Mom the time that I can't. And I give Mom the humor that Rachel can't. Just like good cop/bad cop with me being the good cop. Or something like that.

Brian and our girls, who never faltered one time as we made plans for Nana to move in and live with us, are my favorite people ever. Seriously. I couldn't have picked a better family for myself. I love them more and more and more than that.

My critique group, Gotits, really is a great support group. And we write some super-duper books as well. Thanks much, Christine Jarmola, Jennifer McMurrain, and Marilyn Boone.

My editor, Mari Farthing, didn't even hesitate one tiny second when I asked if her she'd stay on for this project. She also promised to stay on for the next project and the next project and the next one after that. She makes me a better writer and uses as least two pens' worth of red ink on every manuscript. Plus, she's an amazing friend. XO!

I'm grateful to Brandy Walker of Sister Sparrow Graphic Design for working with my awesome-blossom publisher, Road Trip Media, to create this uber-cool book you're holding right now.

And finally, I'm totally grateful for you, my faithful readers. You keep laughing, and I'll keep sharing.

Made in the USA
Middletown, DE
17 June 2023

32753707R00156